Meet Your
Biggest Booster,
Jesus!

Author, Roger W. Gruen
Publisher, Commendations Incorporated
ISBN: 978-0-578-07394-1

Copyright Notices

To Dottie
My Soul-Mate on the
Path to Glory

Preface

You say You have no relationship to Jesus? A storm of thoughts sweep through my mind, and I assert, "Nothing could be further from the truth!" In this book, I detail my convictions, hoping You will be persuaded to develop an intimate relationship with Jesus. Already, Jesus and You have a deep relationship. In fact, everyone on Earth has been profoundly impacted by the One Christians call the Lord Jesus Christ.

Let's begin our discussion with some words about Jesus from the Bible book written by the Apostle John...

> All things were made by Him, and without Him was not any thing made that was made. (KJV John 1:3)

That enormous Sun slipping below the western horizon, those songbirds twittering in the trees, the grassy slope on which You are sitting, the busy roots that are feeding the grass beneath You, and that toddler playing at Your feet; all these were made by Jesus. He and You have a deep relationship. He made You.

It is vitally important that You become aware of the connections between You and Jesus. In this book, we will examine some fundamental concepts that everyone should ponder. Somehow, most earthlings overlook these important themes. They have been fed an erroneous world-view by teachers, books, television programs, movies, magazines, and, even, some celebrities active in the field of religion. We endeavor, herein, with facts and logic, to show You the Truth about Your life and Your destiny.

The word "Gospel" means "Good News". I hope You will end the reading of this book with a Good News view of Your life and its prospects. No one loves You more than Jesus. He created You for a purpose. He wants You to succeed. He is Your Biggest Booster.

Together, let's explore the following six assertions. Each of these is given a full examination in a subsequent chapter of this book. This summary of the topics we will cover is an informal index of the six chapters. In each chapter, the points outlined here are expanded and related to appropriate Scripture passages.

Boost One
Jesus Is Blessing You Now

You are a miracle, an ingenious flesh and blood machine, invented by God, inhabited by a soul and a spirit. The trillions of tiny parts that make up Your body are sustained by God. He is Your life-support system. He blesses You with life, moment by moment. He has placed You into an advantageous social setting. You live in the United States of America, founded on Christian principles and graced by the Church. Therefore, Your social environment advocates high moral standards, monogamy, freedom, the existence of a large middle-class, quality education for all, and scientific research. This mind-set has produced amazing prosperity and fostered charities, service organizations, orphanages, abundant medical facilities, evangelistic movements, missionary programs, and efforts to end slavery, prostitution, and racial discrimination. And, much more. Through Jesus and His Church, Your quality of life is greatly enriched. Jesus is blessing You, now.

Boost Two
Jesus Created You for Heaven

Are You a cosmic accident? a chance offshoot of the "Big Bang"? No, Your body, soul, and spirit are inventions of God, not the result of a mindless sequence of chance occurrences. Those who wish to free themselves from their "Maker" have striven mightily to perpetrate a "hoax" on mankind in the name of Science. "If there is a Maker, I should worship Him", they reason. "If not, I'm free to live without reference to Him or the Bible." They choose the latter course, thinking they are "too smart" to believe the Scriptures. You and I will delve into the question, "How did we come to be?" We will review the ideas of "Young-Earth Christians" and "Old-Earth Christians" and study the mathematical improbability of Evolution. We will see that God did not create "cave men". He created the finest couple that ever lived, Adam and Eve. And, He even created extra-terrestrial beings, residing in Heaven. Jesus made You. He has His eyes set on You. He wants You to be an important part of His Heavenly team.

Boost Three
Jesus Wants to Erase Your Sins and Boost You into Heaven

You and I have a sin problem. Only perfect people can enter Heaven. We are not "good enough" to get in. And, if we are barred from Heaven, we will spend Eternity in Hell. Jesus rescued true-believers from this predicament by taking all the blame for their sins. On the Cross, He took the punishment they deserve for their sins. Their sins were shouldered by Him. His righteousness was poured into them, replacing their unrighteousness. So, believers look forward to a glorious future in Eternity. Jesus wants You to be sin-free, too. You can seek the Lord in prayer and ask Him to erase Your sins. Jesus' Sacrifice can count for You. If

You place Your trust in Him, He will boost You into Heaven when You die.

Boost Four
Jesus Wrote the Bible
to Show You the Way to Heaven

Jesus had You in mind as He instructed holy men of old to write the words that He placed in their hearts. A multitude of detailed predictions were included in the Script, as it was written, over many centuries by dozens of chosen men. One by one, these prophecies have been fulfilled, leading Christians to trust the Holy Book and to anticipate the rest of the events forecasted by it. The Bible is unique among all of the books You might read. It alone reveals the way You should live Your life and prepare for Eternity. It is accurate. Its Message is cohesive. Each of the 66 books ratifies the others. The Bible presents a logical explanation of the human condition, "Who am I? Why am I here? Where am I going?" It is inspiring, because it was written by the One who knows everything; the One who made You and me. And, it is practical. If You follow its advice, Your life will improve. The Bible is God's love letter to You. He wants You to read it and heed it. He wants its Message to Boost You into Heaven.

Boost Five
Jesus Has Created a Reality
Where You May Live
with Him, in Bliss, Forever

A "reality" is a period of time and a place in the Universe where a set of natural laws applies. Here's a list of 9 different realities mankind has or will experience. Some no longer exist, others are yet to come: "Eden", "Pre-Flood", "Pre-Babel", "Here and Now", "Paradise", "Pre-Millennium Heaven", "Hell", "Millennium", and "New Heaven and Earth". You and I are living in the "Here and Now", but we are destined to live in at least 1 other reality. Therefore, it is imperative that You examine what Scientists and Bible-believers say about our present reality and others to come. Scientists are baffled by many phenomena in our present reality. Why can't we travel faster than the speed of light? What causes gravity? Is the whole Universe a weaving of tiny strings? Ironically, modern scientific theories are dove-tailing with ancient predictions found in the Bible. It is thrilling to know that those who reach Heaven will see the full glory of God's handiwork. They will understand the puzzling occurrences of our present era. I hope to see You there, so we can explore the Universe together.

Boost Six

Jesus Wants to Give You a More Abundant Life, Now and Forever

Jesus wants a deeper relationship with You. He wants to give You an "abundant life". To get it, You must become a part of the Family of God. At this very moment, He is knocking on the door of Your heart. He is asking You to be "born again", not physically, but spiritually. If You choose to honor Jesus' wish, You will inherit the treasures stored in Heaven. And, as a down-payment on this future inheritance, the Holy Spirit will take up residence in You. He will comfort You when stress comes your way. He will explain the Bible to You. You will have a blessed assurance that You are saved and Heaven-bound. You will know that Jesus is protecting You, holding You in the palm of His mighty hand. You will learn to pray, frequently. Trouble and heavy burdens will be lifted from You through prayer. You will know that all things are working together for Your good. You will feel Christ's guiding presence. You will stand up for Jesus and draw others to Him. Jesus will Boost You into an "abundant life", now and forever.

Please Note

In some Scripture quotations, I have interjected a word or a phrase to bring out the meaning of the passage as I understand it. These notes have been enclosed in square brackets, "[...note...]", to clearly separate my interpretations from the Holy Writ.

Christians know that there is only one God. But, He has manifested Himself to mankind through three personalities, as the Father, the Son, and the Holy Spirit. The Father is sometimes called the Lord. The Son is often called the Christ, the Messiah and the Lord. And, the Holy Spirit is sometimes called the Holy Ghost or the Comforter. In this text, these terms are used interchangeably.

Boost One
Jesus Is Blessing You Now

Jesus is blessing You personally and socially, at this very moment.

Personal Blessings

In many ways, You are a universe unto Yourself. You live in Your own personal cosmos. You are a living marvel. Every moment You experience is a miracle. You are full of life, an amazing assemblage of living parts. You are about 80 trillion cells. Each of these is a living entity made of hundreds of smaller parts. And, within Your body are about 1600 trillion living microbes. Some of these micro-organisms are helping You survive and some of them are trying to do You in. The structures, mechanisms and maintenance systems in Your body are infinitely more complex than any thing mankind has ever attempted to construct. Only the Lord can keep all this "life" working together harmoniously.

Most of Your cells contain two copies of the "recipe" for Your body. It is unique. God created a specific blueprint for You. It is breathtaking to think that He placed about 160 trillion copies of Your "recipe" in You. If one copy of this plan were printed to paper, it would make a huge book, far more complex than the engineering plans for a skyscraper. All this information is concealed in Your tiny cells.

When You began to grow inside Your Mother, Your embryonic cells carefully followed the "recipe" for You. Think of the information processing involved in the growth and ongoing maintenance of Your body. Every cell needs to know where he is in the grand scheme of the plan and who his neighboring cells are and what their role is. If an adjacent cell dies, a surviving cell looks at the "recipe" and creates a replacement cell and positions it in the proper place. How miraculous is that?

We can imagine a conversation between the cells as an embryo develops. Cell "A" says to cell "B", "Look at the 'recipe'. This is where the heart begins. I will create a cell for this chamber. You work on that valve."

And, when the organs of Your body were completed, who caused them to begin their life-long work? Who caused Your heart to start pumping? Who knew at that moment that Your heart would beat exactly 130,516,212 times? Surely, God is at work here.

However, You are much more than a complex machine. The Bible says You are a composite of a body, a soul and a Spirit. (I Thessalonians 5:23) Your marvelous body is animated by Your soul (Your personality) and Your spirit (Your conscience). Sometimes, in the Bible, the word "soul" is used to refer to both of the invisible body parts, the spirit and the soul. Many books have been written about these entities, but, for sure, no one but God truly understands how these three parts of each human work together.

And, what shall we say of the mind? Myriad thoughts pass through Your brain each day, and God knows them all. Scientists persist in teasing out the way Your mind works, but, largely, it remains a mystery.

The activity in Your body is amazingly complex, yet, with little effort, here You sit reading this book. Your heart is pulsing. Your lungs are breathing. Your eyes are seeing. Your mind is comprehending. Who is in charge of all this activity? God.

Life is a fabulous blessing. Yet, Your dazzling body has its limits. Eventually, its intricate systems will break down. But, Jesus wants to add to the years You will dwell in Your present body better years in a better body that will last forever. He wants to transplant Your soul and spirit into a heavenly body.

The Bible tells us that we live in a cursed world; that things were better in the Garden of Eden, before Adam and Eve sinned. Still, we can see magnificence in God's handiwork. You enjoy the rapturous sounds of passionate music. You delight to the taste of a hot sandwich. You are captivated by the beauty and fragrance of a bouquet of flowers. You are soothed by the buoyancy You feel while playing in a warm pool. Life, with all its problems, has its marvelous blessings.

Social Blessings

Your life intersects with the lives of those around You. Here, too, Jesus is blessing You, now. Can You imagine a world without Jesus? Probably not. Most readers of this book live in the United States, a culture that is greatly influenced by Him. Those unfortunate people living in un-Christian and anti-Christian cultures long for the quality of life enjoyed by You and me, living in a nation shaped by the Christian faith. We have much for which we should be thankful.

Blessings of Christian Influences

Why are Christian influences so invigorating to a culture? Let me explain. Since Jesus began His ministry on Earth, there has always been a body of true-believers we call the "Church". That word has been abused and mis-used. Rightfully, the term should be applied only to those who believe what Jesus taught. Today, this body of believers is the group of souls who study the Bible, believe it, and endeavor to live by its precepts.

The Church has had, and is having, an astounding impact on You. Too easily, we forget the origins of our blessings. But, even a glance at history will tell us that the regions of the Earth that have been touched by the Church are filled with blessings not seen elsewhere. So, You are a recipient of manifold blessings delivered to You by the Church. Why is life so much better in the United States than in many other nations? It is because the Gospel made it to America with enough potency to field a vigorous Church body that has graced our nation with blessings.

Those nations which are now, or once were, in the sway of Christianity are the best places in which to live. This is not a chance occurrence. There is a close correlation between Christian influences and elevated living standards for the common man. And, as we should expect, when nations have drifted away from Christ, that high quality of life, we all desire, has diminished.

I do not mean to imply that there is, or ever has been, a "Christian Nation". Every culture is a mixture of the devout and the debauched. But, many nations have experienced a phenomenon, a "season of Christian enlightenment", that has shaped their institutions and the behaviors of their people. In these swells of belief, we see leaps of progress and great improvements in the life of the ordinary man. There is a connection between the convictions of the citizenry and the quality of life experienced by its individuals.

The Peril of Abandoning Christianity

What happens when a nation abandons Christianity? England is an instructive example. Of course, that nation has done many things wrong and some things right. She has fought immoral wars and, in the past, mistreated some of the natives in her colonies. She has been involved in scandalous and brutal religious quarrels. Still, it is clear that when England experienced a great surge of Christian influence, she became the mightiest nation on Earth. And, simultaneously, she became the center of world-wide, Christian evangelism, taking the Gospel to such far-flung places as Africa, China, India and the Americas. Meanwhile, the British people experienced an enhanced quality of life.

Sadly, the British have turned their backs on Christianity. Their great churches are nearly empty. Many of their clerics are not true Bible-believers. They are simply going through the motions of engrained traditions. And, England is no longer the world force she once was. And, the quality of life in the British Isles has suffered.

Our United States of America is in danger of becoming another such proverb. Even though we were founded by citizens immersed in Christian influences, we have fallen away from our first principles. Corruption in high places is laying waste the concepts enshrined in our Constitution. Anti-Christian sentiment in Hollywood and the broadcast media is denigrating Bible-believers. And, predictably, the welfare of the common man is in jeopardy. While a few elitists are living in extravagance, citizens are having trouble with their jobs and careers. It seems like an economic problem, and it is, but, I believe the real cause of the present diminishment of the American life-style is a wide-spread turning away from Christ.

Still, we live in the best of places. There is a chance that the Church can turn around the attitude of our citizenry. The most patriotic thing we Christians can do is to win people over to the Christian Way. I believe that God is watching our nation from His throne above. He is perfect. He never changes. He is always right, and in II Chronicles He stated His policy concerning the welfare of His people...

> If my people, which are called by my
> name, shall humble themselves, and pray,
> and seek my face, and turn from their
> wicked ways; then will I hear from heaven,
> and will forgive their sin, and will heal
> their land. (KJV II Chronicles 7:14)

If the number of true-believers within our borders increases substantially, we will see tremendous improvements in our nation.

Some would dispute these claims, cataloging the sins of "Christians". Therefore, we need to clarify the fuzzy words, "Church" and "Christian".

The Marks of True Christianity

According to the Scriptures, you are a Christian, a member of the Church Jesus founded, if you hold certain beliefs, such as...

- Jesus is the Son of God.
- Jesus left Heaven to live as a man.
- Jesus was born of the virgin Mary.
- Jesus offered Himself as the Ultimate Sacrifice for your sins.
- Jesus' shed blood washes away all of your sins.
- Jesus rose from the grave, showing that He and you and all His followers have victory over death.
- Jesus founded the Church.
- Jesus ascended to Heaven to prepare a marvelous place in which you and all

> His followers will live with Him,
> forever.

We who are Christians have received an indwelling of the Holy Spirit which helps us live the Christian life. We practice the activities prescribed by the New Testament: Baptism, Communion, Church attendance, caring for the needy, witnessing to the world, and so on. We endeavor to live as Jesus urges us to live. Even so, we still sin at times. We confess our sins to Jesus, and He...

> ...is faithful and just to forgive us our sins,
> and to cleanse us from all unrighteousness.
> (KJV I John 1:9)

Many flippantly claim to be a member of the Church without adhering to these basic doctrines. This has caused great confusion. For instance, once, I was flabbergasted when a Jewish friend of mine stated that Adolf Hitler was a Christian. No! No! Christians believe you must "love your neighbor as yourself". (Matthew 22:39) That directive was not followed by Hitler. Many who wish to denigrate the tremendous success of the Church point to other such villains and label them as Christians.

In addition, some nefarious men and women have claimed to be Church members to improve their opportunities for personal gain. They proclaim Christ as they solicit contributions used to enrich themselves. They pretend to be Christians to get votes. They attend Church to make business contacts. They enter the clergy to obtain an easy job. And so on. Many "Church College" faculty positions, "Church Association" positions, "Church

Denomination Headquarter" seats, and "Church" pulpits are filled by fraudulent "christians".

Blessings You Receive from the Church

If we clear away the flippant and the nefarious riffraff from the Church body, I may safely assert that the Church is a great success. It has had a strong impact on You.

We should not be surprised by the success of the Church. Christ said...
> ...he that believes on me, the works that I
> do shall he do also; and greater works than
> these shall he do... (KJV John 14:12)

Jesus worked great miracles and saved many souls, but He lived in a compact geographic area during a short period of time. He worked with those at hand. Then, He went back to Heaven. He left behind the embryonic Church which grew to do many miraculous works over the entire globe for centuries.

At its onset, the Church was a group of Jews, following Jesus. Due to persecutions emanating from the unpersuaded Jews, Christians began to fan out over the Earth, taking their Judeo-Christian convictions with them. Also, some Christians felt a "call" from the Holy Spirit within them to go "into all the world, and preach the gospel to every creature", as Jesus had directed in Mark 16:15.

Further, we should not be surprised by the incessant resistance the Church faces. Satan is real. He commands an army of wicked spirits. These persistently persuade charlatans to use the auspices of the Church to promote un-Christian messages and deeds. Who has not heard of a "reverend" who doubts the Easter story? How often must we hear of a "pastor" caught in a porn activity? How many politicians have used Christianity as a smokescreen for their wicked behaviors? Satan takes every opportunity to fill men and women with evil spirits and motivate them to use the Church as a tool for fulfilling their lusts. Yet, the Church presses on with backlash from Satan, the "prince of this world", and his devotees. (John 16:11)

History reports that the Church thrived best in Europe, and then touched the European colonies around the world. What happened as the Church marched into new areas? Many things. They are hard to organize into any pattern, precisely because each new Christian received his or her particular gifts from the Holy Spirit. This led Christians into a variety of endeavors. Of course, they all adopted a new standard of morality based on Jesus' command, "Thou shalt love thy neighbour as thyself." (KJV Matthew 22:39)

As Christianity spread, honesty became paramount, greatly improving business transactions. The Church, with its Judeo-Christian ethics, engendered a vibrant middle-class and amazing prosperity. Lifelong monogamy strengthened family units. Christians, wanting their children to be able to read and understand the Scriptures, started schools and schools developed into universities. Some Christians were led to organize programs to care for the elderly and the disabled. Others started hospitals for the sick and injured. The Christians who made it to America put their faith to work in developing the United States, the pre-eminent nation in all of recorded history, with "freedom and justice for all" as its goal. Charities, Service Organizations, and Orphanages were created. Evangelistic Movements, Missionary Programs, and the fight to end slavery and prostitution and racial discrimination emerged.

Now, all these societal improvements were offshoots of dramatic changes within each Christian. When one becomes a Christian, he (or she)...

> ...is a new creature: old things are passed away; ...all things are...new...and all things are of God... (KJV II Corinthians 5:17-18)

We Christians are confident that God is in charge. Kings and nations will all pass away, but God is forever. We have a profound feeling of self-worth, because God loves us, immensely. God sent His only Son to the Cross to take the punishment for our sinful thoughts and behaviors. This wonderful God made us in His image, and He wants each of us to come to Heaven to live with Him, forever.

The efforts of Christians in the early Church ripened into the complex foundations of modern society wherever the Church was allowed to flourish. Fledgling schools became universities. They continued to study God's Bible, but they began to study God's handiwork as well. Science produced the marvelous inventions that are now commonplace. The stronger the Church in a given region, the better the quality of life became.

The Church and the Middle-Class

Have You ever wondered why the USA has a huge middle-class population while many countries have few middle-class citizens? Here's my answer to that question. I believe the strength of the middle-class in any nation is a barometer of the strength of the Church in that nation. If Christianity is widely accepted in a nation, it will develop a large middle-class population. If Christianity is stifled in a nation, the middle-class will be small.

Here's a story that illustrates my point. Probably, You know one of Jesus' commandments, "You should love Your neighbor as You love Yourself." (Matthew 22:39) Let's see how this teaching transformed a small, fictitious town named Calamity. It was down on its luck. The town was depressing. The dwellings were dilapidated. The villagers were suffocated by worries over food and shelter. Calamity had no middle-class. A few rich people held all the assets, tightly. The rest of the citizens were paupers.

Some wise Christians in the next county decided to plant a Church in Calamity. They built an attractive meeting hall and began holding worship services there. They encouraged the citizens to attend. Slowly, the congregation grew. At the urging of his wife, one of the town's employers got involved. As Bill listened to the Gospel sermons, his heart melted. He was saved. He knew he needed to change some of his attitudes and practices. Bill ran a hardware store. He did not pay his employees well. He did not need to. No one in town paid well. But, now, Bill wanted to put Jesus' commandment into action. He raised the salaries of his workers. The results thrilled him. Joe was able to remodel his house. It needed it. Mary made plans to send her son to college. Everyone in his store seemed happier, and the business grew. The best people in town wanted to work for Bill.

Some of Bill's associates complained. They were having trouble finding good help. In fact, some of their best employees had left them to work for Bill. Bill explained, "I gave my heart to Jesus and decided to follow His commandment. I want my employees to have as much as I have. They should have nice housing and food. Their children should have a good education. Jesus' plan is working well for me. Why don't you come to Church and see what you think?" Well, some did, and they followed the path forged by Bill. Others didn't, but even they had to raise wages to attract and retain good employees. The town developed a vibrant middle-class. Over time, some of the middle-class citizens were able to save enough capital to start new businesses and multiply the good found in Jesus' words. Soon, the residents changed the name of the town from Calamity to Hope.

Now, this is just a story, but look around the world and You will see that where Jesus' commandment is known and practiced, a strong middle-class exists. And, where Jesus' commandment is unknown or rejected, the middle-class is very small, and the population is divided into two tiers, the elite and the peasants. Praise God that You live in America, where Jesus' words are honored. And, pray that our people never desert the Christian faith.

You have inherited a treasure. Just because You were born in the United States, You enjoy a very high standard of living. This derives from the courageous efforts of the God-fearing men and women who established this society. Thank God! Yes, Jesus is blessing You now, personally and socially.

Boost Two
Jesus Created You for Heaven

Are You a cosmic accident? the by-product of an alleged primordial explosion? Where did You come from? Why are You on Earth at this moment in history? You have heard answers to these questions from two warring camps. Christians say, "Christ created the Heavens, the Earth, and You." Evolutionists contend, "Science says that there was a 'Big Bang' long ago. It produced the Universe. Spontaneously, life erupted on certain planets, including Earth. Early life-forms evolved into higher creatures, ultimately producing You." To analyze these polar-opposite positions, let's begin by asking the question, "What is Science, and what is Philosophy?"

What Can Science Say?

In Middle-school Science class, You were taught the "Scientific Method". It is stated differently in various textbooks, but it goes something like this:

1. An individual gets a hunch, and proposes an hypothesis.
2. He designs an experiment that would prove to himself the validity of his hypothesis.
3. He performs his experiment and convinces himself that his hypothesis is true.
4. He publishes his results in letters to colleagues or in a scientific journal.

5. Multiple colleagues perform similar experiments, convincing themselves that the hypothesis is true.
6. The hypothesis becomes an accepted scientific fact.

The lesson? We must be cautious with the phrase, "Science says...". Sometimes, it is used loosely. How often have You watched a TV special that featured some of God's intriguing creations and heard the narrator drone, repeatedly, "...Science says that this creature evolved from a pre-historic lizard, which is now extinct..."? Too often! And, it is bad "science". You cannot apply the Scientific Method to something that took place a million years ago, allegedly. Such statements are simply Philosophy. Heavily entrenched Philosophy, I should add.

A Core Issue: How Old Is Planet Earth?

As You study the origin of mankind, for sure, You will note quite different answers to the question, "How old is planet Earth?" Evolutionists and many Geologists believe the planet is billions of years old. They base this notion on "dating systems", which depend on rates of radio-active decay. We'll discuss these methodologies later. Christians, since the early days of the nineteenth century, have vigorously discussed the age of the Earth and how that relates to a correct understanding of the Genesis account of Creation.

"Young-Earth Christians" believe the planet is about 10,000 years old. They believe that the first two verses of the Bible are to be seen as contemporaneous. "Old-Earth Christians" see a huge time-gap between the events of verses 1 and 2...

1. In the beginning God created the heaven and the earth.
2. And the earth was without form, and void; and darkness was upon the face of the deep. And the Spirit of God moved upon the face of the waters.
(KJV Genesis 1:1-2)

"Old-Earth Christians" believe that before the six days of Creation, set forth in Genesis, there was at least one other ecosystem on planet Earth. They believe that many of the bones and fossil imprints we find today are relics of another order of creation that existed in the era of the time-gap between verse 1 and verse 2; that dinosaurs and thousands of other extinct creatures were part of this earlier epoch. They believe this earlier creation perished and Earth "was void" as the six day creative episode began.

"Old-Earth Christians" point to this Bible verse...
These are the generations of the heavens
and of the Earth when they were created,
in the day that the LORD God made the
earth and the heavens...
(KJV Genesis 2:4)
Here, the word "generations" is plural. This implies that more than one generation of life-forms has inhabited this planet.

Further, "Old-Earth Christians" note these words of the Apostle Peter...
...there shall come in the last days scoffers,
walking after their own lusts, And saying,

Where is the promise of his coming? for
since the fathers fell asleep, all things
continue as they were from the beginning
of the creation. For this they willingly are
ignorant of, that by the word of God the
heavens were of old, and the earth standing
out of the water and in the water: Whereby
the world that then was, being overflowed
with water, perished: But the heavens and
the earth, which are now, by the same
word are kept in store, reserved unto fire
against the day of judgment and perdition
of ungodly men. (KJV II Peter 3:3-7)

"Old-Earth Christians" do not think Peter was
referring, here, to the Flood of Noah's time, because
Peter speaks, first, of a "world that then was" that
"perished" and, second, of "the heavens and the
earth, which are now". In Noah's life-time, the
heavens were not replaced. The Earth was radically
changed by the world-wide Flood, but not the
heavens. Yet, Peter points to a time when the
present heavens were created after an earlier
"world" perished. So, if Peter's words do not refer
to the Flood, they must refer to the Creation.
Genesis says "darkness was upon the face of the
deep". Then, God set the sun and moon and Earth
in their current orbits. A new "heavens" system
was established. This interpretation of Peter's
words demands an **"old" use of our planet and a
"new" use. Genesis says that prior to the six**
days of Creation the Earth was "void", suggesting
that it had been inhabited but was, at that moment,
empty of life. Then, God filled the Earth with new
life-forms.

"Young-Earth Christians" believe that all the flora and fauna that have ever lived on Earth were created in the six days described in Genesis. They believe that the bones and fossils are artifacts of ancient life-forms which were destroyed by a variety of events: volcanic explosions, Noah's Flood, and, perhaps, some devastations caused by incoming comets. The dinosaurs may have been killed by the curse God placed on His creation after Adam and Eve sinned or by the Great Flood. "Young-Earth Christians" think the dating systems in use today are not reliable because they are predicated on spurious assumptions about the history of the Earth and the chemistry of its elements and compounds.

Who's right? The question cannot be answered. No one was there to take notes. Let's heed the words of the Lord, spoken to Job...

> Where were you when I laid the
> foundations of the earth? Tell me, if you
> know so much. (NLT Job 38:4)

We are left to ponder the Scriptures and indulge in fascinating discussions with each other. But, You can be certain that all Christians agree with these statements: "God made everything we can touch and taste and see. God made You!"

God's Miracle or Darwin's miracle?

The quarrel between Christians and Evolutionists begins when we examine our planet. What should we make of those old human bones found in Africa? those dinosaur skeletons from China? those layers of rock found in the Midwest? No doubt these are relics of the past. But, piecing these evidences together into a compelling narrative is more like detective work than Science. More than one story may seem to fit the artifacts. This is like forensics. Put a plausible case together and see if the jury believes it.

We Christians believe in miracles. It's easy for us to accept the creation narrative in Genesis. In a robust, flash of creativity, Almighty God made all the flora and fauna we see about us.

Evolutionists believe that life began when a proper chemical brew, pooled in some swamp, was actuated by a natural phenomenon, such as a lightening strike. They say that the primitive life formed in this event gradually mutated into higher life-forms. They spend enormous amounts of time arranging the fossils they uncover into a "tree of life". The tree begins with simple, single-cell organisms and branches into plants and animals of every sort. If a new plant or animal is discovered on a South Pacific island, it is quickly analyzed and placed on some branch of the tree.

When Evolutionists collect fossil imprints that are similar to one of today's animals, they conclude that the present-day creature evolved from the creatures that are depicted in their fossil collection. "But," You say, "there are differences!" "That's right," they say. "As the fossil animals evolved, they improved!" You say, "Can you prove that?" They say, "No, but isn't it obvious? Look, the changes took place over millions of years. No one saw them happen." Finally, You say, "The fact that these fossils look like this present-day animal does not prove that the one came from the other!"

So, we are left with an unprovable "scientific" conclusion. Is this "Darwin's miracle"? Can worms become snakes? Can snakes become birds? Christians say, "No." Evolutionists say, "Yes. But, we cannot prove it." Is this Science or Philosophy? The difference between Creationists and Evolutionists comes down to beliefs. You believe the Bible's record, or You believe the claims of the Evolutionists, who preface their assertions with their favorite phrase, "Science says..." Personally, I believe...

>...the Lord made heaven and earth, the sea, and all that in them is...
>(KJV Exodus 20:11)

The Evolutionists have a belief system, an orthodoxy, much like that of a religious cult. They want You to believe their teachings. They evangelize in our classrooms.

Someday We Will All Agree

Evolutionists express various opinions. Some are atheists. Others claim to be Christians who cannot accept the whole Biblical narrative. Some are nominal "christians" who say, "Jesus was a nice fellow who said some nice things." Others reject Jesus completely, but still believe there is a deity out there, somewhere. And, some believe in "Evolution guided by the hand of God".

On the darkest side of this belief spectrum are those

Evolutionists who oppose the Biblical explanation of how we came to be in order to eliminate God from their contemplations about the origin and meaning of life. They want to live a worldly lifestyle. They do not want to have any obligation to worship our Maker and follow His commandments. They are the heathen portrayed in Psalm 2...

> Why do the heathen rage, and the people imagine a vain thing? The kings of the earth set themselves, and the rulers take counsel together, against the LORD, and against his anointed, saying, Let us break their bands asunder, and cast away their cords from us. He that sitteth in the heavens shall laugh: the LORD shall have them in derision. (KJV Psalm 2:1-4)

Evolutionists of this ilk want to sever all connections to a divine Maker, "break the bands asunder" and "cast away the cords". They cling to any notion that eliminates the sovereignty of God over their lives. In a dreadful way, this rebellion against God is laughable from God's perspective. Look at it this way. Let's suppose that You created a life-like robot. And, an awed admirer of Your creation asked it, "Who made You?" And, it answered, "No one. There was a big explosion and somehow I took shape." Well, we would all laugh. But, that is the logic of those who deny a divine Maker. I hope that You never embrace this Philosophy, because those who hold to it are headed for a rude awakening on Judgment Day. The Apostle Paul wrote...

> ...we shall all stand before the judgment seat of Christ. For it is written, As I live, saith the Lord, every knee shall bow to me, and every tongue shall confess to God. So

34

then [Paul reasoned] every one of us shall
give account of himself to God.
(KJV Romans 14:10-12)
Now or later, You will believe that Jesus created
You. If You come to this conclusion now and
become a Christian, Your glorious future in Heaven
is assured. Do not wait till later.

The Debate

Let's review other arguments put forth by
Evolutionists and Christians as they debate.

Don't the fossils prove Evolution? No, they prove
that a massive, crushing force trapped living things
in muck that has turned to rock over the years.
Would not the Flood of Noah's day have done this?
The highest mountains were covered with water.
Today, the highest mountain is Mount Everest. It
rises about 6 miles above sea-level. If You have
ever lugged a five-gallon bucket of water, You
know that water 6 miles deep would have
tremendous crushing force.

Keep this in mind. What is taught in high schools
and colleges is usually "old news". New theories
are proposed and popularized and, belatedly, reach
classrooms where they are taught as fact. Then, the
popular theories are debunked, but teachers and
professors continue teaching what they were taught
when they were schooled. A gap of twenty to forty
years separates the leading edge of investigation
from what is being advocated in the classroom. So,
it is with the "Big Bang" theory. It is commonly
taught as fact in our schools, but recently, leading
Cosmologists, Scientists who study the origin and

nature of the Universe, have modified the theory. And, so it is with fossils. Numerous leading life-science professors, today, are questioning the commonly accepted meaning of the fossil record. It does not support the gradualism of species change that Evolution predicts. The notion that fossil "A" became fossil "B" which became fossil "C", and so on, seems to exist only in the mind of the beholder, not in fact. But, teachers and professors are still teaching the old theme of the gradual Evolution of life-forms.

By the way, when Scientists began to advocate a beginning of the Universe, such as the "Big Bang" theory, they took a step in the direction of Biblical belief. The Bible says the Universe has a beginning. During the many centuries preceding the appearance of the "Big Bang" theory, many scholars argued that the Bible was wrong. They insisted that the Universe had always existed in its present form; it had no beginning. Now, at least, we all agree. The Universe had a beginning. I like to think of it this way: There was no Big Bang -- the Lord whispered and the Universe leapt into existence.

What the fossils do show is the amazing diversity of species created by God. Whatever else You might think of God, You must admit He is creative. In the fossil imprints we see many species that do not exist today. Did these species become extinct in an age that pre-dated Adam? or when the world was cursed after Adam sinned? Were they killed by the change in the environment of the Earth as it passed from the pre-Flood ecosystem to the post-Flood? We cannot say, but the fingerprints of God's handiwork are inscribed in stones which are scattered all over the globe.

The Improbability of Evolution

Shortly after Charles Darwin proposed the theory of Evolution, some Mathematicians objected. They realized that if the theory was true, the world must have existed for a very long time. Here is why. The laws of probability tell us that if two events must occur to produce a satisfactory outcome, the likelihood that the outcome will be realized is the product of the probability that each event will occur. For example, the probability that a single coin toss will yield a "head" is 1 out of 2, or 1/2 or 50%. The probability that 2 consecutive coin tosses will both yield "heads" is 1/2 times 1/2, or 1 out of 4, or 1/4 or 25%.

Now, suppose You are at a paint store, blindfolded, facing a display of a 1000 color cards and You throw a dart at the display. What are the odds that You will hit "Sahara Sand"? The answer is 1 in a 1000, or 1/1000 or .001. And, the odds You could hit the same color with 2 consecutive throws is 1/1000 times 1/1000, or 1 in a million.

Now, let's consider the human eye, having thousands of parts. Evolutionists say that each of these parts developed by a series of chance mutations. Let's focus on the pupil. Basically, it is a beautiful muscle. Its duty is to control the amount of light entering the eye. Too much light is blinding. Too little, and visualization is difficult. The pupil is composed of millions of cells that must work together. First, let's concentrate on the muscle cells responsible for regulating the size of the pupil opening. When the incoming light is too strong, they must lengthen their shape to make the opening smaller. When the incoming light is weak, these same cells must compact their shape to dilate the opening. Second, other cells form a control system that judges the light intensity and sends a signal to the muscular cells, "Lengthen" or "Tighten." Third, there are cells involved in supplying blood flow to the pupil, to nourish each of the cells and to remove the waste products they excrete after they metabolize their nutrients. It is a very sophisticated system. All of the parts of the system must be in place for the system to be useful. And, the array of cells must be in a circular pattern to form a perfect opening in the pupil.

How did all these components and systems come to be? Christians say, "God fashioned the eye with ease, placing each of the diverse cells of the pupil in its proper place and training them to perform their functions." Evolutionists say, "The pupil was developed over hundreds of millions of years. Long ago, by chance, some organism was born with a light-sensitive cell. Being superior to his brothers and sisters, he survived longer and spread his good fortune to many offspring. One of them, by chance, was born with a transparent cell covering his light-sensitive cell. And, in turn, one of his offspring, by chance, was born with a cluster of light-sensitive cells, covered by a cluster of transparent cells. Gradually, the whole eyeball developed. Then, a creature was born with some tissues centered on the transparent surface of the eyeball. Over time, by chance, these morphed into the modern pupil."

The imagined chain of events leading to a workable pupil is very long. The descriptive story of these events reminds us of an endless, children's story, such as, "How the Leopard Got His Spots". Each event on the chain has only a very slight chance of occurrence. A Mathematician attempting to calculate the probability that the evolutionary story is true must multiply each of millions of fractions, like 1/200000, times each of the other fractions. The result is that the likelihood that the pupil was created by such a process is 1 in a "gazillion". No wonder, Mathematicians were quick to object to Darwin's theory of Evolution. The Mathematicians concluded that the theory was highly unlikely, and, if, indeed, it was true, the processes involved must have taken a very long time.

And, we must ask, "Why did these myriad changes take place, one at a time, in such a way that, finally, each human has a wonderful pair of eyes?" In and of themselves, most of these changes would not have improved the eye of the sub-human species that preceded modern mankind. Only when all the changes were in place could high-quality, three-dimensional vision have occurred. So, what prompted the first of the myriad changes? Who developed the master plan and set each improved cell in exactly the proper position? Evolutionists say it all happened by trial and error. Christians say, "God invented it and manufactured it in seconds."

How Accurate are Dating Systems?

The Evolutionists were not deterred by the arguments put forth by Mathematicians. They

insisted, "The god of chance put the eye together."
And, a host of college professors said, "Amen."

Out of necessity, the Evolutionists constructed a
"dating" system to bolster their case. They
arranged fossils in a logical pattern from less
complex to more complex and began to assign
"dates" to various life-forms, assuming that the less
complex gradually mutated into the more complex.
Then, they developed various dating systems which
they calibrated to their expectations. So, today if
You ask to have a bone or rock dated, You will get
an answer that fits their world-view. Their dating
systems were designed to give the answers they
want. Their "logic" is quite circular.

Curiously, most dating systems are calibrated by
using a rate of radio-active decay. As radio-active
elements expel their "loose" particles, they become
a daughter element. For example, uranium decays
to become lead. Evolutionists make the strange
assumption that when the Earth was formed by God
or the "Big Bang", present-day uranium-lead
mixtures were pure uranium. This is just a wrong-
headed assumption! If enough uranium is found in
a concentrated mass, a nuclear explosion erupts.
So, the Lord did not form pure uranium rocks. Yet,
Evolutionists calculate the age of our planet by
projecting backward from a rock's current uranium-
lead mixture to when the rock contained only
uranium and no lead, allegedly.

Also, please ponder why the Evolutionists arrange
the various species in an ascending order. Do they
believe that the "god of chance" is also a "god of
purpose"? That would be contradictory. But, they

believe the "god of chance" methodically produced higher and higher life-forms until it crowned its efforts with the creation of men and women.

Incidentally, though it may surprise You, I believe we should teach Evolution to Christian students. But, we should state that it is an unprovable theory. Life-scientists have used this theory to develop classifications for all life-forms. If one does not know the theory, it is impossible to understand many valuable books.

Old Bones

What about ancient bones? Remember this: bones can be re-shaped rather easily by applying water and heat. Probably, You have seen the process while watching a TV special on headhunters. Sometimes, the natives demonstrate how they shrink the skulls of their victims. That is why it is surprising to see well-educated men trying to draw "proof" from a few human bones found in some wilderness. How old are they? What chemical processes have they endured?

Recently, I read a speech by an anthropologist who had uncovered a few bones. From them, he created a story for his fellow Scientists. He was convinced that the creature stood about four feet tall and was a very good runner. Is this Science or science-fiction? In truth, the bones may not be as old as he claimed. Moisture and heat may have shrunk them. The skull may have been distorted by pressures surrounding it.

We cannot rely on dating systems to tell how long this creature laid there. If we were to place several sets of bones on a table with no notes about where they were found or when, Evolutionists would be hard-pressed to assign an age to each set. Different teams of scholars would offer wildly differing age values. If You take an interest in life-science journals, You will note that the experts have vigorous debates about dating artifacts.

Common Components

Recently, it has become fashionable for Evolutionists to argue, "Look! All living things have common components. Is it not clear that they all came from a common ancestor?" For instance, on August 6, 2010, the AFP, a world-wide news agency carried this story...

> Mankind may be descended from apes but Australian scientists have found proof of links much closer to the sea floor, with a study revealing that sea sponges share almost 70 percent of human genes.

Well, this does not prove that sponges and humans evolved from a common ancestor! It proves that God used common components to make each of His creatures. We humans adopt the same strategy as we build houses. Tiny, inexpensive cottages are made from such things as plywood, lumber and nails. So are mansions.

It's obvious that dogs and cats share more common components than do an elephant and a salmon. But, this just shows what the Almighty did with various collections of atoms and molecules and cells.

What Did God Create?

We cannot begin to enumerate the whole of it.
Mankind has not yet plumbed the depths of many
orders of creation. Deep in the sea, thousands of
life-forms exist that we have never seen.
Thousands of other life-forms have gone extinct.
Depending on which botanist you ask, there are
25000 to 30000 different orchids in our rain forests.
How many have You seen? Scientists studying ants
estimate that there are 12000 to 20000 species of
ants. How many have turned up at Your house?
Those who study sea life estimate there are more
than 20000 different life-forms in the oceans. Push
a shovel into the soil in Your backyard, and lift out
the dirt. In there are thousands of living creatures.
Most have never been named or studied. Also, the
Bible speaks of extra-terrestrial life; heavenly
angels and trees and beautiful creatures unlike those
on Earth. And, there may be some form of life
elsewhere in the Universe. We know so little. We
have only examined a minute portion of God's
handiwork.

However, logic and the Bible teach us that the most
impressive creatures on this planet are men and
women, and that includes You. Have You ever
considered how remarkable Adam and Eve were?
They were the only perfect humans ever to exist on
Earth. They were the most intelligent persons in
history. They were the best looking man and
woman in all the ages. They were athletic. Their
bodies were designed to live forever. They were
quite different from the dreary "cave men and
women" hypothesized by our intelligentsia.

When Adam and Eve sinned, the perfection all about them was cursed by God. Every thing in creation was marred by the curse. Adam and Eve were cursed. Imperfections were introduced into their bodies. They, like You, were now on the way to death. Their children did not receive a perfect start in life. The DNA they inherited was flawed. And, so it was with every living thing on Earth. All the flora and fauna were damaged. Grasses died. Horses died. All the savage behavior we note on Earth was unleashed. Believers groan for the day when they shall enter the new Paradise that Jesus has created for His followers. (Romans 8:23)

Why did God create?

God is a social being. The Godhead is three Persons in One. These three Personalities converse with each other. God has a history of creating living entities to share His magnificent presence. We read, in the Bible, of beautiful creatures that surround God's throne.

Before God created man, He created the angels. Their history is complex. We shall not analyze it here, but we have noted some of the relevant Bible passages in this brief overview. Angels were created in Heaven. That is their natural estate. Unlike us, they do not procreate. (Matthew 22:30) Each angel was created by God. Like us, they are creatures of free-will. Even though they had always lived in the presence of the Godhead, some of the angels sinned. They became very prideful and chaffed at the idea that God had absolute authority over them. One of the most impressive angels was Lucifer. (Ezekiel 28:11-19) He organized an anti-

44

God movement. He wanted the other angels to worship him instead of the true God. (Isaiah 14:12-17) One-third of the angels were drawn into his rebellion. (Revelation 12:4) God exiled these rebels to planet Earth. (Revelation 12:7-9) Here, Lucifer is known as "Satan" or the "Devil", and the other wicked angels are called "evil spirits" or "demons".

Sometime after He created the angels, God decided to make another kind of creature...

> ...God said, "Let us make mankind in our image, in our likeness, so that they may rule over the fish in the sea and the birds in the sky, over the livestock and all the wild animals, and over all the creatures that move along the ground." So God created mankind in his own image, in the image of God he created them; male and female he created them. (NIV Genesis 1:26-27)

We are not smart enough to fully comprehend what God meant by these words, but let me offer an observation. The Apostle John taught that when we Christians get to Heaven and see Jesus, we will be like Him...

> Dear friends, now we are children of God, and what we will be has not yet been made known. But we know that when Christ appears, we shall be like him, for we shall see him as he is. (NIV I John 3:2)

So, it seems that we are made like the "Son" Personality of the Godhead. The "Father" is a spirit, the "Spirit" is a spirit, so we must be like the "Son". God decided that we humans should begin our existence on Earth with an option for Heaven. We were given a free-will to worship Him or to not worship Him. Alternatively, He could have made us robots that had no choice but to worship Him. Why did He not choose to do that? Think the idea through. If You had to choose between having a robotic child who would always mind You and always give You a sweet hug as he traipsed off to bed at the precisely defined time or a child of free-will who would show You love when he was so inclined, which would You choose? The free-will child might not hug You and might not obey You on all occasions, but when he did, You would appreciate it, because the love would be voluntary, not pre-programmed.

God did not create You on a whim. He created You, with a free-will, in the hope that You would ask Him to be Your best Friend; in the hope that You would come to live in a magnificent place He has prepared, Heaven. But, He ruled that everyone in Heaven would be there because they had freely chosen Him to be their Lord. He knew the majority of the human race would reject Him and malign Him. Some would even crucify Him. And, these wicked, immortal beings would be assigned a torturous, future role at some level of Hell. God has offered to save such souls from their eternal punishment, but they have spurned His offer.

God wants to Boost You into Heaven. In fact, He would be pleased if everyone chose Him, but He knew from the beginning that would not happen. He has done everything necessary for You to make it to Heaven. He has given You life. He has given You a way to shed Your sins and become qualified for a position in Heaven. He is Your Biggest Booster.

Boost Three
Jesus Wants to Erase Your Sins and Boost You into Heaven

Like everyone else, You and I have a serious problem. Only sin-free people can get into Heaven. For sure, we are not "good enough" to go there. Jesus solved that problem for those of us who put our trust in Him. He took all the blame for our transgressions. All our shame was shouldered by Him on the Cross. He endured the punishment we deserve. The Apostle Paul put this thought into a letter he wrote to Christians living in Corinth...

> ...[God] made him [Jesus] to be sin for us,
> [Jesus, the very One] who knew no sin;
> [so] that we might be made the
> righteousness of God in [and through] him
> [Jesus]. (KJV II Corinthians 5:21)

At the Cross, Jesus' righteousness was poured into us who believe He died for us, even as our sins were poured into Him. He completely removed our sins from us. Therefore, we confidently look forward to a glorious future in Eternity. Jesus is urging You to trust in Him, too. He wants to Boost You into Heaven and keep You out of Hell.

The Penalties for Sin

To better understand how Jesus' death, long ago, on a hill called Calvary, can Boost You into Heaven, we must examine God's plan for saving sinners from experiencing eternal banishment to Hell. Sinners have broken God's rules. They deserve punishment for their rebellion against the wishes of Almighty God. In fact, the Bible teaches...

...the wages of sin is death...

(KJV Romans 6:23)

The proper "payoff" for sin is a death sentence; spiritual death here and now, followed by a subsequent Eternity in Hell. But, God loves mankind so much that He gave each individual a way to escape these penalties for sinful thoughts and behaviors. He decided to let a "substitute" suffer the punishment we deserve. As we shall see, our "Ultimate Substitute" is Jesus. He died in our place.

The First Sin

How this "Salvation by Substitution" plan was instituted is a gripping story. It began in Eden. How long Adam and Eve lived in the Garden before their first sin ushered in a crushing curse upon themselves we cannot say. They had perfect, ageless bodies. They were beautiful people in a magnificent Paradise. They lived in complete safety and comfort. They were the most athletic and intelligent people ever to grace planet Earth. They were direct creations of God. There was not one thing wrong with them. On every side they saw perfection. The flora and fauna were without fault.

48

The sky was splendid. Nothing in their environment ever withered or died.

Would You not love to see a documentary on what life was like in Eden? No violence. All the animals played together in harmony. No noisome insects. No fear. A deer would let You come near. Birds would not flush as You approached them. Unlike today, it never rained. There was an underground irrigation system that put forth a morning mist that watered the plants. (Genesis 2:5-6)

God was a frequent visitor to the Garden. The Bible informs us that God presents Himself to mankind in three ways, as the Father, as the Son of God, and as the Holy Spirit. So, God is often called "The Trinity". This triune nature of God is somewhat analogous to a glass of iced water, sitting in a warm room. Here You perceive water molecules presented in three ways, as liquid water, as solid ice and as water vapor in the surrounding air, condensing on the sides of the glass. The Scriptures tell us that the Father aspect of God is a spirit. The Holy Spirit aspect of God is always referred to as a spirit. So, the aspect of God that walked and talked with Adam in the Garden was the Son of God. We think of Him as Jesus, since that is what He was called when He came to Earth in New Testament times.

Adam and Eve were sin-free. There was one and only one way they could sin. Jesus gave them just one rule; they were not to touch or eat the fruit of the "Tree of the Knowledge of Good and Evil". Jesus had said, "If you break this law, you will surely die." (Genesis 2:17)

Now, as we mentioned earlier, Satan had been cast from Heaven to Earth. He was not pleased to see this beautiful pair enjoying the blessings of God while he was suffering in God's scorn. So, he attacked Eve. Just as Satan is persistently urging You to sin, so he tempted Eve. He twisted Jesus' words. He alleged that Jesus was mean. He claimed that eating the forbidden fruit of the tree would make her wiser and more perceptive and would not cause her to die. He persuaded Eve to break the one rule Jesus had given her. Then, she convinced Adam to join her in the transgression. In Genesis, we read...

> Eve said to the Devil-possessed serpent, "It's only the fruit from the tree in the middle of the garden that we are not allowed to eat. God said, 'You must not eat it or even touch it; if you do, you will die.'" "You won't die!" the serpent replied to the woman. "God knows that your eyes will be opened as soon as you eat it, and you will be like God, knowing both good and evil." The woman was convinced. She saw that the tree was beautiful and its fruit looked delicious, and she wanted the wisdom it would give her. So she took some of the fruit and ate it. Then she gave some to her husband, who was with her, and he ate it, too. (NLT Genesis 3:3-6)

Echoes of Eden

Today, You and I face many temptations. And, each of them reminds us of the one faced by Adam and Eve. God says, "Thou shalt not steal." Satan says, "God will not hold You accountable for swiping that candy bar. He should not deprive You of such a tasty treat." God says, "Thou shalt not commit adultery." Satan says, "God will not hold You guilty for sleeping with that alluring person. It will be wonderful." God says, "Thou shalt not lie." Satan says, "God will not send You to Hell for making false and deceptive statements." And, like Eve, we all seek companions in our crimes. "Let's both steal a candy bar." "Let's make love." "Let's make up an alibi to cover our lies."

To Adam and Eve, to You, and to me, Jesus says, "The wages of sin is death." (Romans 6:23) Satan says, "That is ridiculous. That's way too harsh! Jesus would never follow through with that threat." Satan wants You to sin and to join him in Hell. The last thing he wants is for You to go to Heaven where he can never again dwell. But, Jesus wants You to join Him in Heaven. The battle of the ages is on. Which side will You choose?

It is difficult for You and me to grasp the holiness of God, since we are sinful creatures. But, God will not associate with any wickedness, small or large. Every sin is an insult to God. Still, He wants You and me to befriend Him and come to dwell with Him. But, we cannot do that if we are stained by our sins. As we noted, earlier, Satan was evicted from Heaven, because He maintained that he was at least equal to God. He even persuaded other angels to worship him. God would have none of that nonsense. He kicked Satan and the wicked angels that followed him out of Heaven. So, You can see that God will not let us come into His holy realms with any tinge of sin. One unforgiven sin is enough to keep us from the eternal Paradise.

The Terrible Curse

Though it is preposterous to think that I know the Contemplations of Almighty God, let me take a crude stab at how God viewed the sin crisis in Eden...

> This lovely couple and their future offspring will sin, because they have the free-will to do so. I want them to love me and live in Paradise with me and keep my laws voluntarily. I do not want to remove their free-will. But, I must evict them from this Paradise. Therefore, I will set up a future Paradise. Some of mankind will go there when they die, the ones who love me and follow my instructions. I will give each man and woman a way to be set apart from the sins they commit, to be sin-free again. Those who avail themselves of my remedy will be admitted to the new Paradise. But, henceforth, life here on Earth will be rigorous. I will place a severe curse on the Earth and its creatures. Those men and women who believe in me will I protect as they endure the woes of this world. I will cause them to enter the future Paradise.

The curse fell abruptly and profoundly. Suddenly, Adam and Eve knew they were naked. They scrambled to cover their flesh with fig leaves, sewn together. For the first time, they were afraid of Jesus. When He came to visit, they hid among the trees. Their guilty hearts felt fear. Jesus got them to confess and laid out the ramifications of their transgression.

Eve would begin to bear children. She would have a romantic desire for her husband. She and her female offspring would have great pain in childbirth. Her husband would have ascendancy over her.

Adam would have to work hard all the days of his life to provide for himself and his family. The ground would be cursed. It would bring forth thorns and thistles. Adam would earn his bread "in the sweat of his face". (Genesis 3:19) He would have a strong, romantic desire for Eve.

No longer would all of the Earth's creatures be vegetarians. Some of them would now be predators, killing other creatures and devouring them. Even Adam and Eve would begin to kill animals, roast them, and eat their meat.

Adam and Eve would have to leave Eden. After a tough life in a cursed world, they would die. Jesus had said, "If you eat of that tree, you shall die." But, in love, Jesus said He would create another Paradise. They could go there when they died, if they followed His new plan for the salvation of sinners. During the many years they would live on Earth, they would need to confess their sins to

Jesus, frequently, and have the stain of their sins removed by a system of "Substitutionary Sacrifice".

Substitutionary Sacrifice

Jesus demonstrated what He meant. He selected an animal, probably a lamb. He told them that the animal selected for a sin sacrifice must be a male that was the first-born offspring of his mother. And, he must be free from any blemishes or deformities. Then, Jesus had them place their hands on the head of the ram and pray that their sin would be transferred to the lamb. Then, He shocked them. He took a knife and slit the throat of the ram. Blood poured forth as the ram slumped to the ground. Adam and Eve were sickened by the sight. "Is this how bad sin is?", they thought. They had never seen any plant wither or any creature die. Now, because of their sin, a beautiful ram lay at their feet in a pool of blood.

Jesus taught them, "Without the shedding of blood there is no remission of sin. This ram has died in your place."

> ...without the shedding of blood there is no forgiveness [of sin]. (NIV Hebrews 9:22)

Then, Jesus showed them how to dress the ram and offer it as a Substitutionary Sacrifice for their sin, roasting the flesh. He had them eat meat for the first time, remembering that the ram's blood was shed to lift the stain of their sin from them.

Further, Jesus showed them how to use the hide of the ram to make apparel. He made them coats of skin. Adam and Eve were quick learners. They

54

were brilliant. So, they understood the grim lessons that Jesus taught them. Having thus instructed them about the way their lives would proceed, Jesus evicted them from Eden.

Remorse

How different everything was East of Eden. Now, Adam and Eve noticed that some of the animals were acting in menacing ways. They observed certain creatures stalking others, killing them, and devouring their flesh. Life was radically different. How they missed the comforts and tranquility of Eden. Gone were those intimate conversations with their Creator. They recalled how He described the six days of Creation, the workings of the underground irrigation system, the movements of the moon, and so much more. They had hung on every word that came from His lips. Everything had been splendid. Now, everything was wrecked.

Adam and Eve had much to learn. Adam spent hours fashioning tools that would help him till the ground. He decided to keep weapons such as a spear and a large knife handy to defend against vicious bears and lions and wild dogs. He managed to domesticate the more docile creatures such as cattle, horses and sheep. He devised ways to catch fish.

Eve learned to forage for wild berries and fruits and nuts. What had been so simple in Eden was much more difficult now. Especially, she despised the chiggers that attacked her in the berry patches. She devised a way to raise chickens and became an accomplished cook of their meat and eggs.

How they both missed the Garden! How they
longed for the future Paradise Jesus had promised!
How they missed Jesus' frequent visits! They could
feel His presence when they prayed. They felt close
to Him when they offered sacrifices for their sins.
But, in many ways, God seemed to have slipped
behind a veil.

Soon, babies arrived. Some of the crudeness of
their new life-style was masked by the joy of seeing
little ones that reminded them of each other. Early
on, they brought forth Cain and Abel. Many
brothers and sisters followed. They recounted to
these little ones how things had been in the
Garden of Eden. They told them of their first sin
and why they had been evicted. Most of all, they
emphasized that Jesus would let them live in a new
Paradise when they died, if they would follow His
salvation plan. When their children sinned, they
showed them how to confess their sins and offer a
Substitutionary Sacrifice to God.

Cain Rejects God's Rules

Most of the offspring of Adam and Eve accepted
their teachings. Some did not. The Bible tells us of
a time when Cain and Abel met to offer sin
sacrifices to God...

> ...Cain presented some of his crops as a
> gift to the LORD. Abel also brought a gift
> — the best of the firstborn lambs from his
> flock. The LORD accepted Abel and his
> gift, but he did not accept Cain and his gift.
> This made Cain very angry, and he looked
> dejected. "Why are you so angry?" the

LORD asked Cain. "Why do you look so dejected? You will be accepted if you do what is right [and follow my commandments concerning sacrifices for sins]. But if you refuse to do what is right, then watch out! Sin [in the persons of Satan and his evil spirits] is crouching at the door [of your heart], eager to control you. But you must subdue it [Satan's influence] and be its master." One day Cain suggested to his brother, "Let's go out into the fields." [Abel pleaded with him to repent and obey the Lord.] And while they were in the field, Cain attacked his brother, Abel, and killed him. (NLT Genesis 4:3-8)

Cain broke the rules his parents had taught him. He was angry when God would not accept his offering. He knew it was not a proper Substitutionary Sacrifice. It was not a first-born male of the flock. He could not eat the flesh of his offering and thank God for accepting its death in place of his. The fruit of the ground that he offered could not bleed and fulfill the maxim, "Without the shedding of blood there is no remission of sin."

The Prophetic Nature of Substitutionary Sacrifices

Why was the Lord so insistent that the rules be followed? Jesus knew the end from the beginning. The Trinity had designed the Substitutionary Sacrifice system to point to Jesus' Substitutionary Sacrifice on the Cross of Calvary. For centuries, the animal sacrifice system would prepare

earthlings for the Sacrifice of Jesus. When they saw
Jesus' perfect Sacrifice, they would comprehend its
meaning. John the Baptist, the great New
Testament prophet, was keenly aware of the
Substitutionary Sacrifice system. At the beginning
of Jesus' ministry, John pointed to Jesus and
proclaimed...

> ...Look, the Lamb of God, who takes away
> the sin of the world! (NLT John 1:29)

After Jesus was Crucified, the early believers
understood that He had given Himself up as the
Ultimate Sacrifice for the sins of all believers. The
Substitutionary Sacrifice system was complete. No
further sacrifices were to be made. Instead, true-
believers, in prayer, would confess their sins to
Jesus, mentally place their sins on Him, and His
death would suffice to remove their sins from them.

Perversions of the Sacrifice System

Cain was the first to pervert the Substitutionary
Sacrifice plan, but many others have done it, too.
As You read through ancient history, You will
picture people offering sacrifices to all manner of
idols. Many offer inappropriate items, just as Cain
did. But, the fact that they were sacrificing to some
alleged deity is testimony to the authenticity of the
events recorded in Genesis. The worst perversions
were those rituals in which humans were sacrificed.

Even today, as You tour the world, You will see
"worshipers" making animal sacrifices. I recall
seeing a missionary film in which a witchdoctor, in
South America, was sacrificing a tropical bird to
one of his deities. I read, recently, of a ceremony
conducted by some Indonesians before they dived

into the China Sea to seek sunken treasures. They
roasted a cock in honor of some sea-god. In
November, 2009. The Guardian, a British paper,
reported a huge animal sacrifice event in Nepal.
The "worshipers" offered bulls, killing more than
250,000 animals as part of a Hindu festival in the
village of Bariyapur, near the border with India.

Yes, Adam and Eve thoroughly imprinted the need
for Substitutionary Sacrifices for sins into the
human psyche, but sinful man corrupted the practice
by breaking the rules set forth by Jesus.

The Trail of Blood in History

Centuries passed. Gradually, mankind put the Lord
out of their thoughts. Most ignored the rules that
had been given to Adam and Eve. But, a small
number of believers clung to the teachings of the
Lord. By the time of Noah, mankind had become
so wicked that only eight souls were followers of
God: Noah and his wife, their three sons, Shem,
Ham and Japheth, and the sons' wives. God
shepherded them all into the ark they had built to
save them from a world-wide Flood that killed
every other human.

They remembered God's rules. When they stepped
off the ark...
> ...Noah built an altar to the LORD, and
> there he sacrificed as burnt offerings the
> animals and birds that had been approved
> for that purpose. (NLT Genesis 8:20)
Once again, every human on Earth was a believer,
and each of the eight understood the Substitutionary
Sacrifice system.

Many years later, Abraham was called by God to move into the land of the Canaanites. When he arrived there...

> The LORD appeared to Abram and said,
> "To your offspring I will give this land."
> So he built an altar there to the LORD,
> who had appeared to him.
> (NIV Genesis 12:7)

Abraham was selected by God to be the father of the Judeo-Christian family. He and his progeny perpetuated the Substitutionary Sacrifice system through the many centuries of history leading up to the Substitutionary Sacrifice of Jesus on the Cross. We read of sacrifices being made by Isaac and Jacob. Moses, under God's aegis, formalized a complex system of sacrifices for sins, and other sacrifices to give thanks to the Lord. David, Solomon and the Old Testament prophets were diligent in following God's rules for Substitutionary Sacrifices.

True-believers chose their sacrifice victims carefully. They selected a first-born male without blemish from their flocks. Jesus was the first-born male from Mary's womb, and He lived His life without a moral blemish. True-believers spilled the blood of their sacrifice victims. Jesus' blood was spilled at His Crucifixion. True-believers consumed the flesh of their victims, thanking God for letting the death of the animal suffice for the death they deserved for violating God's rules.

Since the Cross, in remembrance of the Ultimate Sacrifice that was made to erase our sins, we Christians frequently re-enact the ceremony instituted by Jesus at His "Last Supper" before His suffering. We consume bread and wine. The bread reminds us of the body of Jesus that was offered in our place. The fruit of the vine reminds us of the horrific shedding of Jesus' precious blood. We are freed from all our sins by this Great Substitutionary Sacrifice. Jesus died in our place. He erased our sins. Being sin-free, now, we are fit for Heaven.

Jesus wants You to be sin-free, too. You can address the Lord in prayer and ask Him to erase Your sins. Jesus' Sacrifice can count for You. If You truly place Your trust in Him, He will Boost You into Heaven when You die.

Boost Four
Jesus Wrote the Bible to Show You the Way to Heaven

Jesus, the Father, and the Holy Spirit had You in mind as They instructed holy men of old to write the words that They placed in their hearts. The Bible is unique among all of the books You might read. It alone reveals the way You should live Your life and prepare for Eternity. The Bible is God's love letter to You. Your Heavenly Father wants You to read it, and heed it. He wants it to Boost You into eternal bliss.

The Apostle Paul exhibited the attitude that true-believers have toward the Bible in one of his letters to a young preacher named Timothy...

> ...from infancy you have known the Holy Scriptures, which are able to make you wise for salvation through faith in Christ Jesus. All Scripture is God-breathed and is useful for teaching, rebuking, correcting and training in righteousness, so that the servant of God may be thoroughly equipped for every good work. In the presence of God and of Christ Jesus, who will judge the living and the dead, and in view of his appearing and his kingdom, I give you this charge: Preach the word; be prepared in season and out of season; correct, rebuke and encourage — with great patience and careful instruction. (NIV II Timothy 3:15-4:2)

I hope You will come to believe as Paul did. We Christians are sure that the Scriptures lead us to faith in Christ Jesus. That faith saves us from an Eternity in Hell. We are certain that the Scriptures were inspired by God. We study the Bible, because it prepares us to live the Christian life of "good works". We long for the promised Second Coming of the Lord, who will judge the "living and the dead" when He returns to Earth to set up His Kingdom.

What is Your opinion of the Bible? Do You revere it? Have You studied it? By sharing with You my thoughts about the accuracy of the Bible, I hope to encourage You to trust the Holy Book. I feel challenged as I write. I can only present the facts as I see them. If You are convinced, it will be due to the supernatural efforts of the Holy Spirit.

Why do I believe the Bible is a Message from God to my heart? The reasons are many. They are sprinkled throughout this book. Here is a concise list of what gives me confidence in the truth of the Scriptures:

1. The Bible is historically accurate. Though it is a compilation of the writings of many believers over many centuries, its assertions are right. Archaeologists and Historians probe its depths. They examine its every word for clues to the events and geography of ancient times. And, they have proved it to be a valid fountain of information. It has led them to excavate many of the sites documented in its pages. The artifacts and

writings they have found corroborate the Scriptures.

2. The Bible Message is cohesive. The writers do not contradict each other. No, they present a consistent theme. The writings of each author re-enforce the Messages of the others. A multitude of detailed predictions were included in the Scriptures. One by one, these prophecies have been fulfilled, leading Christians to trust the Holy Book and to anticipate the rest of the events forecasted by it. The Apostle Peter wrote...

> ...prophecy never had its origin in the human will, but prophets, though human, spoke from God as they were carried along by the Holy Spirit. (NIV II Peter 1:21)

3. The Bible presents a logical explanation of the human condition. Pagan philosophers have toiled to promote other theories of the existence and purpose of God's creation, but their work seems hollow when compared to the Message of the Bible.

4. The Bible is inspiring. It is an extension of the Lord. He understands You and me. He knows every thought we have. The author of the book of Hebrews stated this opinion well...

> ...the word of God is quick [alive], and powerful, and sharper than any twoedged sword, piercing even to the dividing

asunder of soul and spirit, and of
the joints and marrow, and is a
discerner of the thoughts and
intents of the heart.
(KJV Hebrews 4:12)

5. The Bible's recommendations work. Life
is better when we heed the Bible's
commandments. As we compare Christians
to unbelievers, we see that Christians are
healthier, happier, live longer, and are eager
to see what the future holds. They are
confident that they will have a blessed
Eternity.

Let's consider how the Bible helped to shape one of
the greatest men in history. The Apostle Peter was
a prophet. He taught that Christ would return to
Earth, someday, and reign over the entire planet.
His confidence in this idea was bolstered by his
understanding of Old Testament Writings. We can
grasp his view of the Bible by analyzing the
following passage. He wrote to his Christian
readers...

All praise to God, the Father of our Lord
Jesus Christ. It is by his great mercy that
we have been born again, because God
raised Jesus Christ from the dead. Now we
live with great expectation...
(NLT I Peter 1:3)

Note that Peter praised God that each true-believer
is "born again". That's why Christians say, "We
live with great expectation. Jesus came back from
death; so will we!"

Peter added details of the "great expectation". When we who are true-believers die, we will come...

> ...into an inheritance that can never perish, spoil or fade. This inheritance is kept in heaven for you [Christians], who through faith are shielded by God's power until the coming of the salvation that is ready to be revealed in the last time.
> (NIV I Peter 1:4-5)

By the power of God, we Christians are kept ready to receive our salvation. It is reserved in Heaven for us. It will be revealed at the "last time". Keep in mind that true-believers are "saved" at the moment they come to belief. Here, Peter spoke of the ultimate ramifications of true belief. The "saved" will receive the completion of their salvation in the "last time".

Presently, we Christians rejoice in anticipation, even though we are buffeted by the troubles of this era...

> So be truly glad [Christians, Peter advised]. There is wonderful joy ahead, even though you have to endure many trials for a little while. These trials will show that your faith is genuine. It is being tested as fire tests and purifies gold — though your faith is far more precious than mere gold. So when your faith remains strong through many trials, it will bring you much praise and glory and honor on the day when Jesus Christ is revealed to the whole world. (NLT I Peter 1:6-7)

Also, Peter knew that our steadfastness in Christ would bring praise and honor and glory to Jesus when He comes to reign.

All our dreams of eternal bliss will come true when Jesus returns. Peter continued...

> You [Christians] love him [Jesus] even
> though you have never seen him. Though
> you do not see him now, you trust him; and
> you rejoice with a glorious, inexpressible
> joy. The reward for trusting him will be the
> salvation of your souls.
> (NLT I Peter 1:8-9)

We Christians have never been as happy as we will be when we see Jesus.

What were the foundations of Peter's belief in this glorious future? First, he was a follower of John the Baptist. Second, he was the foremost Apostle of Jesus, during His earthly ministry. And, third, Peter trusted the Old Testament Scriptures, implicitly. As he wrote of the magnificent salvation that God had prepared for Christians, Peter stated...

> Concerning this salvation, the prophets,
> who spoke of the grace that was to come to
> you [Christians], searched intently and
> with the greatest care, trying to find out the
> time and circumstances to which the Spirit
> of Christ in them was pointing when he
> predicted the sufferings of the Messiah and
> the glories that would follow.
> (NIV I Peter 1:10-11)

Peter alluded to the many passages in the Old Testament that had predicted the sufferings of Christ and Christ's triumph over death. And, note, Peter believed that the Spirit of Christ was in those prophets who wrote their statements centuries before Jesus lived among us and died for us.

Further, Peter said, those prophets...

...were told that their messages were not for themselves, but for you [Christians]. And now this Good News has been announced to you by those who preached in the power of the Holy Spirit sent from heaven. It is all so wonderful that even the angels are eagerly watching these things happen. So think clearly and exercise self-control. Look forward to the gracious salvation that will come to you when Jesus Christ is revealed to the world. (NLT I Peter 1:12-13)

Peter noted that the Old Testament prophets had set forth in advance many of the things that he and other Gospel preachers declared to the world, aided by the Holy Spirit as they spoke, and that, even the angels were quite interested in their sermons. Peter urged Christians to "think clearly", to prepare their minds for the task of sharing the Gospel. He asked Christians to "exercise self-control" as they discussed the grace that will be poured out on all Christians when Jesus comes again.

Christ divides history. True-believers in the Old Testament era looked forward to Jesus. We look back. But, every soul who makes it to Heaven will have been saved by Christ's Great Sacrifice. The Old Testament saints pre-viewed the Cross in their animal sacrifices. God blessed their solemn offerings, allowing them to suffice as Substitutionary Sacrifices for their sins. Today, true-believers look back to the Ultimate Sacrifice at the Cross. We assemble at the Communion Table in remembrance of Christ's sufferings.

There is great continuity in the Message of the Bible. We see this as we compare the writings of the Old Testament, looking forward to Jesus, and the writings of the New Testament, looking back at Jesus. There are thousands of prophecies in the Bible. Some scholars claim there are 2500 to 3000 of them and that 2000 have been fulfilled already. But, to make my point, that the Scriptures are reliable, let us focus on three major prophetic themes. First, let's look at prophecies about Israel. Second, prophecies about Jesus coming to Earth to suffer and to die for sinners. And, third, prophecies about the End-Time, when Jesus will return to reign over the whole Earth. Hopefully, discussing these three themes will convince You that the Bible is the most important manuscript ever penned. The fulfilled prophecies prove its accuracy. Therefore, You should trust its advice on how to live "Here and Now" and how to prepare for Eternity.

Why do Bible students compile different counts when they enumerate the prophecies? Because, some "prophecies" are not fulfilled for centuries while others are fulfilled immediately. For instance, in a passage found in John, chapter 9, Jesus made a little clay from the earth at His feet and applied it to a blind man's eyelids. He told the man to go to the pool of Siloam and wash his face and he would be able to see. The man went to the pool and washed and received his sight. Now, was Jesus prophesying in this case? Some say yes, some, no. But, no matter how they count them, all serious Bible readers agree that thousands of Bible prophecies have come true.

Israel and the Babylonian Captivity

Israel is the subject of many prophecies. Some of the most intriguing concern the years in which a large number of Jews were captives in Babylon. Isaiah was the first prophet to see the Captivity coming. In a passage that spoke of many great things that God would do for Israel, suddenly, Isaiah spoke of a man named "Cyrus", a man who is famous in history. He was a mighty Persian king. However, Cyrus was not yet born when Isaiah wrote of him. In fact, Cyrus was born about 150 years after Isaiah wrote his book.

Recording words given to him by the Holy Spirit, Isaiah saw the Lord saying...
> "When I say of Cyrus, 'He is my shepherd,' he will certainly do as I say. He will command, 'Rebuild Jerusalem'; he will say, 'Restore the Temple.'"
> (NLT Isaiah 44:28)

As Isaiah wrote these words, Jerusalem was intact, as a strongly walled city, and the Temple, built by King Solomon, was in fine shape. Since Isaiah predicted that a fellow named Cyrus would give orders that Jerusalem and the Temple should be built, his prophecy implied that at some point, in the years between Isaiah's prophecy and the days of Cyrus, the city and the Temple would be destroyed.

From other portions of the Old Testament and from secular history, we know that a Babylonian king named Nebuchadnezzar ruined Jerusalem and the

Temple and took many Jews to Babylon as slaves. Later, Cyrus conquered Babylon, and he was used by God to return the Jews to Judah. Amazingly, Isaiah saw part of this history well before it happened. Isaiah's prophecy went further...

> This is what the LORD says to Cyrus, his anointed one, whose right hand he will empower. Before him, mighty kings will be paralyzed with fear. Their fortress gates will be opened, never to shut again. This is what the LORD says: "I will go before you, Cyrus, and level the mountains. I will smash down gates of bronze and cut through bars of iron. And I will give you treasures hidden in the darkness — secret riches. I will do this so you may know that I am the LORD, the God of Israel, the one who calls you by name. And why have I called you for this work? Why did I call you by name when you did not know me? It is for the sake of Jacob my servant, Israel my chosen one. I am the LORD; there is no other God. I have equipped you for battle, though you don't even know me, so all the world from east to west will know there is no other God. I am the LORD, and there is no other. (NLT Isaiah 45:1-6)

We can only wonder how stunned Cyrus must have been when one of his advisors, a man named Daniel, showed him this prophecy about 180 years after Isaiah had recorded it. Daniel was, also, an Old Testament prophet. He had been forced to go to Babylon by Nebuchadnezzar when he was a young man. Over the years in captivity, Daniel had acquired a reputation as a wise man of God. He served in Nebuchadnezzar's court and then in

Cyrus' court. We can almost hear Cyrus exclaim, "How did that ancient prophet know my name, long before I was born?" Daniel must have explained to him the great accuracy of the Scriptures. Cyrus let everyone in his kingdom know of this prediction. As Isaiah said, everyone from the East to the West heard of Isaiah's prophecy. Hopefully, You, too, are impressed by this uncanny prediction from the pages of the Bible.

This miraculous, historic episode gains importance as we read from the book written by Jeremiah. He was another prophet of God. He lived in Israel just prior to the beginning of the Captivity. He saw it coming...

...the LORD Almighty says this: "Because you [Israel] have not listened to my words, I will summon all the peoples of the north and my servant Nebuchadnezzar king of Babylon," declares the LORD, "and I will bring them against this land and its inhabitants and against all the surrounding nations. I will completely destroy them and make them an object of horror and scorn, and an everlasting ruin. I will banish from them the sounds of joy and gladness, the voices of bride and bridegroom, the sound of millstones and the light of the lamp. This whole country will become a desolate wasteland, and these nations will serve the king of Babylon seventy years. But when the seventy years are fulfilled, I will punish the king of Babylon and his nation, the land of the Babylonians, for their guilt," declares the LORD, "and will make it desolate forever."

(NIV Jeremiah 25:8-12)

From other passages in the Bible, we know that the Jews had, indeed, not "listened" to God's words. In this passage Jeremiah lamented that fact. By the lifetime of Jeremiah the Jews had long since decided to disobey the sabbatical rules set forth by God. God had told them to let the land they farmed lay fallow every seventh year, and, after seven sabbatical years, to celebrate a "Year of Jubilee", letting the land lay fallow for another year. By the time of the Captivity, Israel had skipped seventy sabbatical years. For that reason, God kept them in Captivity for seventy years. Jeremiah predicted the duration of the Captivity in advance.

The inspired historian who wrote the Second Book of Chronicles explained the Captivity in this way...

> The few who survived were taken as exiles to Babylon, and they became servants to the king and his sons until the kingdom of Persia came to power. So the message of the LORD spoken through Jeremiah was fulfilled. The land finally enjoyed its Sabbath rest, lying desolate until the seventy years were fulfilled, just as the prophet had said.
> (NLT II Chronicles 36:20-21)

Isn't that amazing? Jeremiah foretold the length of the Captivity. And, he re-iterated his prediction in another passage...

> ...the LORD says: "You [Israel] will be in Babylon for seventy years. But then I will come and do for you all the good things I have promised, and I will bring you home again." (NLT Jeremiah 29:10)

Somehow, Daniel, still in Captivity in Babylon, obtained a copy of Jeremiah's book. He commented in his own book...

> In the first year of Darius son of Xerxes (a Mede by descent), who was made ruler over the Babylonian kingdom — in the first year of his reign, I, Daniel, understood from the Scriptures, according to the word of the LORD given to Jeremiah the prophet, that the desolation of Jerusalem would last seventy years.
> (NIV Daniel 9:1-2)

The end of the Captivity was detailed in the opening verses of the book written by another prophet, Ezra...

> In the first year of Cyrus king of Persia, in order to fulfill the word of the LORD spoken by Jeremiah, the LORD moved the heart of Cyrus king of Persia to make a proclamation throughout his realm and also to put it in writing: "This is what Cyrus king of Persia says: 'The LORD, the God of heaven, has given me all the kingdoms of the earth and he has appointed me to build a temple for him at Jerusalem in Judah. Any of his people among you may go up to Jerusalem in Judah and build the temple of the LORD, the God of Israel, the God who is in Jerusalem, and may their God be with them. And in any locality where survivors may now be living, the people are to provide them with silver and gold, with goods and livestock, and with freewill

offerings for the temple of God in
Jerusalem.'" (NIV Ezra 1:1-4)

So, the Temple and Jerusalem were re-built by the
Israelites when they returned from Babylon. The
new Temple was reconstructed from the ruins of the
"First Temple", which was built under the
supervision of the famous Jewish king named
Solomon. The reworked Temple is often referred to
as the "Second Temple".

Centuries after the "Second Temple" was
completed, a ruthless king known as "Herod the
Great" updated it. Allow me to say a word about
this vile man. Probably, You have heard that this
Herod was the king who received the "wise men"
who came from the East, shortly after Jesus was
born. Herod heard from them that a "King of the
Jews" had been born. He summoned Bible scholars
and asked them if they knew where the Messiah
was to be born. The scholars indicated that the
prophet Micah had given the Messiah's birthplace as
Bethlehem. Soon after the "wise men" visited Jesus
and returned to their own country, Herod ordered
that all boys 2 years old and under, in the environs
of Bethlehem, be killed. Jesus was spared, because
Joseph, his step-father, had been warned in a dream
to flee to Egypt with his wife and Son. This
"Second Temple", as updated by Herod, was the
one Jesus visited, often, when He was on Earth.
Yet, in Jesus' day, a bit of Solomon's Temple
remained. We read of Jesus teaching in a portion of
the Temple called "Solomon's Porch".

Israel and the World-Wide Dispersion

So, You see, the destruction of Jerusalem, and its reconstruction, was foretold by Hebrew prophets. These events occurred centuries before Jesus came to Earth. But, a second destruction of Jerusalem, an even more complete devastation of the city and the Temple, was, also, predicted by the prophets. That destruction came after Jesus had left Earth and ascended to Heaven. It occurred in 70 A.D. A Roman general named Titus sacked the city and completely dismantled it. He buried the remains of the city and planted crops on top of the heap. He arrested any surviving Jews he could catch and sold them into slavery, dispersing them throughout the ancient world.

The Old Testament contains hundreds of prophecies about the destruction of Jerusalem. To separate those that refer to the first destruction, about 6 centuries before Christ, from those that refer to the second destruction in 70 A.D. is a very complex task. We will not do that in this text. But, let me show You one ancient prophecy that surely refers to the devastation wrought by Titus. It was written down over 700 years before it was fulfilled...

> Listen to me, you leaders of Israel! You hate justice and twist all that is right. You are building Jerusalem on a foundation of murder and corruption. You rulers make decisions based on bribes; you priests teach God's laws only for a price; you prophets won't prophesy unless you are paid. Yet all of you claim to depend on the LORD. "No harm can come to us," you say, "for the LORD is here among us." Because

of you, Mount Zion will be plowed like an
open field; Jerusalem will be reduced to
ruins! A thicket will grow on the heights
where the Temple now stands.
(NLT Micah 3:9-12)

Micah spoke of a time when Israel would be so
corrupt that honest judgment would be hated and
fairness would be perverted. The signs described
by Micah remind us of the days when Jesus walked
the Earth. Micah said that the leaders of Israel, in
that day, would murder and do wicked deeds to
enhance their power. We are reminded of the
leaders who shed Jesus' blood, without just cause.
Micah said that the judges of that time would be
bought with bribes and that the priests and the
"prophets" of that day would favor those who paid
them money. All the while, they would claim that
God was on their side, protecting their interests.
Again, we are reminded of Jesus' days on Earth.
Assuredly, Micah was speaking of Jesus' era.
About 40 years after Jesus was crucified, Titus de-
constructed Jerusalem and the Temple. He heaped
earth on the remains, plowed the city as a field, and
planted a crop upon it.

Jesus echoed the prophecies of Micah and other Old
Testament prophets. In Matthew we read...

Jesus left the temple and was walking
away when his disciples came up to him to
call his attention to its buildings. "Do you
see all these things?" he asked. "Truly I
tell you, not one stone here will be left on
another; every one will be thrown down."
(NIV Matthew 24:1-2)

In Luke, we read more of Jesus' predictions about the impending destruction of Jerusalem. He said...

...this is the time of punishment in fulfillment of all that has been written [in the Old Testament]. How dreadful it will be in those days for pregnant women and nursing mothers! There will be great distress in the land and wrath against this people. They will fall by the sword and will be taken as prisoners to all the nations. Jerusalem will be trampled on by the Gentiles until the times of the Gentiles are fulfilled. (NIV Luke 21:22-24)

Also, in Luke, we read...

...As he approached Jerusalem and saw the city, he wept over it and said, "If you, even you, had only known on this day what would bring you peace — but now it is hidden from your eyes. The days will come upon you when your enemies will build an embankment against you and encircle you and hem you in on every side. They will dash you to the ground, you and the children within your walls. They will not leave one stone on another, because you did not recognize the time of God's coming to you." (NIV Luke 19:41-44)

So, Jesus declared that Jerusalem would be devastated because its citizenry did not acknowledge His visitation. They had rejected their Messiah.

What Micah had predicted 700 years in advance and Jesus had predicted 40 years ahead came true. Are

You impressed? I hope so. The accuracy of the Bible is uncanny, because it is inspired!

The Bible predicted the destruction of Jerusalem by Nebuchadnezzar and the destruction of Jerusalem by Titus, followed by the dispersion of the Jewish people into the nations of the ancient world. Jews were scattered into every corner of the Earth, but, somehow, they maintained their identity as Jews. Unlike other clans that have been forced into slavery and flung to widely scattered regions and have inter-married and been absorbed by the people of their new homelands, the Jewish people clung to their traditions and culture and remained distinct. Even today, they maintain their identity. That, too, fulfills prophecy, for the Bible has long predicted that, at some moment in history, the Jews would return to Palestine. As we noted earlier, Jesus said...

> Jerusalem shall be trodden down of the Gentiles, until the times of the Gentiles be fulfilled. (KJV Luke 21:24)

Jesus gave no date for when "the times of the Gentiles" would be fulfilled, but the word "until" in His prediction implied that "the times of the Gentiles" would come to an end, someday.

Many other prophecies recorded in the Bible stated that the Jews would, someday, return to the promised land and re-establish their nation. For instance, Isaiah said...

> ...the Lord will reach out his hand a second time to bring back the remnant of his people — those who remain in Assyria and northern Egypt; in southern Egypt, Ethiopia, and Elam; in Babylonia, Hamath,

and all the distant coastlands. He will raise
a flag among the nations and assemble the
exiles of Israel. He will gather the scattered
people of Judah from the ends of the earth.
(NLT Isaiah 11:11-12)
And, Isaiah added this Message from God...
Do not be afraid, for I am with you; I will
bring your children from the east and
gather you from the west. I will say to the
north, 'Give them up!' and to the south,
'Do not hold them back.' Bring my sons
from afar and my daughters from the ends
of the earth... (NIV Isaiah 43:5-6)

Jeremiah joined the theme, recording these words of
the Lord...
...I will gather the remnant of my flock out
of all countries whither I have driven them,
and will bring them again to their folds;
and they shall be fruitful and increase.
(KJV Jeremiah 23:3)

And Ezekiel heard this Message from God...
...I will take you [Israel] from among the
heathen, and gather you out of all
countries, and will bring you into your own
land. (KJV Ezekiel 36:24)

Today, these Old Testament prophecies are being
fulfilled. Late in the nineteenth century, a few Jews
founded the "Zionist Movement". They began to
urge Jews from every sector of the globe to move to
their old homeland. The movement gained traction,
slowly at first, but as the two world wars scourged
Europe and anti-Semitism reached obnoxious
proportions, the movement accelerated. Finally,

in 1948, the United Nations passed an official declaration that created the modern Jewish state. Just as the Bible had predicted for thousands of years, Israel existed again.

Christians have watched these developments with great interest, for the Bible predicts that some "End-Time" events, near the Second Coming of Jesus to Earth, will take place in a Jewish Temple in Jerusalem. For nearly 2000 years, there has been no Temple there. So, we who believe the Bible must conclude that the Jews will soon fulfill the "End-Time" prophecies and build a Third Temple.

The Bible says that an enormously important event will transpire in this new Temple. During the "End-Time" a wicked dictator will rule over the whole world. The Bible calls him the "Antichrist". About 3 and 1/2 years before Christ returns to set up His world-wide Kingdom, according to the Apostle Paul, the Antichrist...

> ...will exalt himself and defy everything
> that people call god and every object of
> worship. He will even sit in the temple of
> God, claiming that he himself is God.
> (NLT II Thessalonians 2:4)

As You may suspect, God will have none of this insolence. You will see, in the next chapter of this book, how God will defeat and deal with this loathsome man.

Messianic Prophecies

Many of the Bible's prophecies speak of the life and times of Jesus. Some scholars count nearly 500 predictions, others, less. But, for sure, the Jews were expecting the Messiah when Jesus was born as a babe in Bethlehem. We will not make an exhaustive review of all the Messianic prophecies here. Many wonderful books have been written on the subject. But, I want to mention enough Messianic predictions for You to see the amazing accuracy of the Scriptures, in the hope that You will come to trust them.

Psalm 22

About 1000 years before Jesus was born, one of his ancestors, King David, wrote a Psalm that contains any references to the Passion of Christ. Just think of it! This song was in Israel's hymnal for a 1000 years, and, then, the events it foretold occurred. This is awesome! Here are the first eighteen verses of this song, Psalm 22. I have interrupted the text, occasionally, offering explanatory comments...

My God, my God, why have you forsaken
me? Why are you so far from saving me,
so far from my cries of anguish?
(NIV Psalm 22:1)

Probably, You know that as Jesus hung on the Cross, He quoted from this verse, "Why have You forsaken Me?". Jesus was God in human flesh. The God aspect of Jesus had determined that it was necessary that He die as the Perfect Sacrifice, covering all the sins of all true-believers. Still, the human side of Jesus was depressed. He felt God had deserted Him. He felt forsaken.

My God, I cry out by day, but you do not
answer, by night, but I find no rest.
(NIV Psalm 22:2)

When Jesus was nailed to the Cross, the skies were

83

brightened by the sun. But, about noon, for 3 hours, a supernatural darkness enshrouded the globe. It was like night, but sinister. There was no light at all. Candles and torches would not ignite. An absolute curse of darkness prevailed. It terrified everyone. It was as if all humanity was blind. No one wanted to move, for fear of falling.

During this blackout, all the sins of all true-believers of all times were laid on Jesus, and when He died, those sins died with Him. It was too hideous for anyone to see. God turned off the light.

You have felt the pain of sin. Your heart jumped in Your chest when You saw the lights of the police car following You and when the officer charged You with speeding. You broke into a hot sweat when Your parents caught You in a lie. Perhaps, You have a disease or an injury caused by Your past transgressions. Yes, sin causes mental and physical pain. Now, imagine how Christ felt in those dark hours when all the sins of all believers were poured into Him. The human side of Jesus agonized under the weight of all those sins. But, as Jesus took them on, He conferred His righteousness on each believer who trusted in His Sacrifice. As the Apostle Paul put it: God...

> ...made him [Jesus] to be sin for us, [Jesus, the very One] who knew no sin; [so] that we might be made the righteousness of God in [and through] him [Jesus]. (KJV II Corinthians 5:21)

There is a miraculous time-warp in this horrid, yet wonderful, dark moment. This exchange of Jesus' righteousness for the sins of believers was for humans of all times. It forgave the sins of Adam and Eve. It forgave the sins of Abraham and Sarah. It forgave the sins of David. It forgives the sins of believers of our era, and it will forgive the sins of believers yet to be born. Today, You may reach back into time and space and give Your sins to Jesus. He will give You His righteousness in return.

> Yet you [Father] are enthroned as the Holy
> One; you are the one Israel praises.
> (NIV Psalm 22:3)

Even God did not want to see those awful 3 hours when Jesus took the punishment of sinners on Himself. The Holy Father turned away from the gruesome sight. He remained in the realms of Heaven.

> In you our ancestors put their trust; they
> trusted and you delivered them. To you
> they cried out and were saved; in you they
> trusted and were not put to shame. But I
> am a worm and not a man, scorned by
> everyone, despised by the people.
> (NIV Psalm 22:4-6)

Jesus, the man, meditated on His situation. Generally, God is responsive to the needs of His devout followers. But, Jesus was in pain, on the Cross, dying for sinners, and He received no relief. For His punishment to count, it had to be real. Jesus pondered Words that He Himself had used to describe the appearance of the lost souls who inhabit Hell. (Mark 9:43-46) He cried, "I am a worm!" Remember, the Scriptures say "the wages of sin is death." (Romans 6:23) Jesus experienced death on behalf of all those He saved by His Great Sacrifice. Then, He visited Hell, briefly, to throw off the load of sin He had assumed on the Cross. (Psalm 16:10)

> All who see me mock me; they hurl
> insults, shaking their heads. "He trusts in
> the LORD," they say, "let the LORD
> rescue him. Let him deliver him, since he
> delights in him." (NIV Psalm 22:7-8)

The New Testament Gospels recount the events cataloged in these verses. Most of those who thronged to see the Crucifixion jeered at Jesus.

> Yet you brought me out of the womb; you
> made me trust in you, even at my mother's
> breast. From birth I was cast on you; from
> my mother's womb you have been my
> God. (NIV Psalm 22:9-10)

Jesus meditated upon His humanity. Truly, He was a man.

> Do not be far from me, for trouble is near
> and there is no one to help. Many bulls
> surround me; strong bulls of Bashan
> encircle me. Roaring lions that tear their
> prey open their mouths wide against me.
> (NIV Psalm 22:11-13)

Jesus, as God, was determined to finish the duty of the Cross. But, Jesus, the man, was enraged by the phony dignitaries who came to gloat over His murder. They reminded Him of the prize bulls of the region called Bashan that were groomed and decorated for sale as top-tier sacrificial animals. These wicked spectators were elite, well-dressed priests and politicians and scholars and military men. They surrounded Him as He grimaced in pain. They saw the woeful scene as a vindication of their world-view. They thought, "This peasant from Galilee is where he belongs!" They were in triumph. Jesus was in torments. Satan, their guiding, evil spirit, was rejoicing within them. Satan, "the ravening and roaring lion" (I Peter 5:8), was in possession of their thoughts. He made this moment, the most vile event in human history, seem like sweet justice to these brute beasts.

> I am poured out like water, and all my
> bones are out of joint. My heart has turned
> to wax; it has melted within me. My mouth
> is dried up like a potsherd, and my tongue
> sticks to the roof of my mouth; you lay me
> in the dust of death.
> (NIV Psalm 22:14-15)

What a horrid picture of Crucifixion! When David wrote this Psalm, crucifixion had not yet been conceived. A millennium later, the Romans were using it all over their empire. Yet, David describes it vividly. Jesus, the man, felt as useless as a smashed pot. He knew that His Great Good Deed had brought Him to this moment of death.

> Dogs surround me, a pack of villains
> encircles me; they pierce my hands and my
> feet. (NIV Psalm 22:16)

How savage did it get? Stray dogs were hungrily seeking the blood of Jesus. Wicked bystanders were excited by the distress of the Savior. And, amazingly, David saw Roman soldiers nailing Jesus to the rugged Cross a thousand years before it happened.

> All my bones are on display; people stare
> and gloat over me. They divide my clothes
> among them and cast lots for my garment.
> (NIV Psalm 22:17-18)

As Jesus hung for hours, His skin was stretched ever more tightly over His chest. He could see His rib cage protruding. While He endured, the Roman soldiers parted His garments and gambled for them.

I hope that this discussion of Psalm 22 has caused You to grasp the magnificence of the Scriptures. Only God could have placed these details in the mind of David well before the time of their fulfillment. Truly, King David was led of the Lord to pen these words. But, he was not the only one to see the Passion of Christ in advance.

Isaiah's Predictions

The prophet Isaiah lived about 700 years before Christ. Yet, he wrote some detailed predictions about the sufferings of the Messiah during the Passion. He quoted, in advance, the thoughts of Jesus...

> I offered my back to those who beat me,
> my cheeks to those who pulled out my
> beard; I did not hide my face from
> mocking and spitting. (NIV Isaiah 50:6)

Just as Isaiah forecasted, Jesus was flogged, and some of the soldiers who tormented Him yanked strands of His beard from His cheeks, and some of His enemies spit on Him in derision.

And, Isaiah saw that the Jews would be sharply divided in their opinions about Jesus. Some would seek to make Him their King, especially on Palm

Sunday, at the beginning of Passion Week. Isaiah predicted, Jesus...

> ...shall be exalted and extolled, and be very
> high. (KJV Isaiah 52:13)

But, in his next sentence, Isaiah spoke of how the Roman soldiers would batter Jesus, a few days later...

> ...many were amazed when they saw him.
> His face was so disfigured he seemed
> hardly human, and from his appearance,
> one would scarcely know he was a man.
> (NLT Isaiah 52:14)

Isaiah saw more ugly details of the way Jesus would be abused. Speaking as if he was present at Calvary, in chapter 53, verses 3-12, Isaiah said...

> He [Jesus] was despised and rejected — a
> man of sorrows, acquainted with deepest
> grief. We turned our backs on him and
> looked the other way. He was despised,
> and we did not care. Yet it was our
> weaknesses he carried; it was our sorrows
> that weighed him down. And we thought
> his troubles were a punishment from God,
> a punishment for his own sins! But he was
> pierced for our rebellion, crushed for our
> sins. He was beaten so we could be whole.
> He was whipped so we could be healed.
> (NLT Isaiah 53:3-5)

Isaiah captured, in his prophecy, the ambivalence of Jesus' disciples as Jesus died for them on the Cross. It was a woeful scene. A few days earlier, Jesus had made a triumphal entry into Jerusalem. Now, He was despised and rejected. Many of His disciples were afraid to show themselves openly. They hid, when they should have been praising Him for the Great Work He was finishing for them. Remember, this Ultimate Sacrifice was offered to erase the sins of those of us who are true-believers; to help us shoulder the griefs we encounter in this cursed world; to succor us in times of sorrow. But, at the time of Christ's suffering, most of His followers were morose. Jesus seemed to be smitten by God. In truth, He was taking the punishment we deserve for our sins. We are healed by His wounds.

> All we like sheep have gone astray; we
> have turned every one to his own way; and
> the LORD hath laid on him the iniquity of
> us all. (KJV Isaiah 53:6)

You and I are like wayward sheep. Our flesh, the world, and the Devil have, at times, driven us away from God. Jesus is the cure for our rebellion. If we have placed our trust in Christ's Sacrifice, all our iniquities have been laid on Him and erased from our record in the Book of Life.

> He [Jesus] was oppressed and afflicted, yet
> he did not open his mouth; he was led like
> a lamb to the slaughter, and as a sheep
> before its shearers is silent, so he did not
> open his mouth. (NIV Isaiah 53:7)

The love of Jesus for His devotees caused Him to adopt a passive approach to His arrest and trial and murder. Had He wished, He could have halted His arrest. At other times, He had walked unscathed through crowds who hated Him. He could have won the court to His point of view with His superior wisdom. He could have caused Pilate to release Him. He could have walked away from His torturers. He could have healed Himself and descended from the Cross. But, He loved those

90

who loved Him and those who would come to love Him. He determined that He would take on Himself the punishment His followers deserved.

> Unjustly condemned, he [Jesus] was led away. No one cared that he died without descendants, that his life was cut short in midstream. But he was struck down for the rebellion of my people. (NLT Isaiah 53:8)

Of course, Jesus had no wife and no children. By His death and His divinity, He was cut off from producing offspring. Yet, in a greater sense, He became the Head of the Family of God. Spiritually speaking, we who believe are children of the King, Jesus. We are the "people" for whom Jesus was "struck down".

> He [Jesus] had done no wrong and had never deceived anyone. But he was buried like a criminal; he was put in a rich man's grave. (NLT Isaiah 53:9)

It is uncanny that Isaiah saw Jesus' grave-site so many centuries in advance. A portion of Calvary Hill was a graveyard for the elite of Jewish society. The rich paid great sums of money to be buried there. Their tombs were caves carved in the rocky hill. Prominent Jewish leaders, who had become followers of Jesus, Joseph of Arimathaea and Nicodemus, took the body of Jesus from the Cross just before sunset. Joseph had prepared an elegant tomb for himself in the Calvary Hill Cemetery. He elected to bury Jesus in his own tomb. So, as Isaiah had predicted, Jesus died as a criminal but was buried in a rich man's grave.

> But it was the LORD's good plan to crush
> him [Jesus] and cause him grief. Yet
> [Isaiah says, quoting God] when his life is
> made an offering for sin, he will have
> many descendants. He will enjoy a long
> life, and the LORD's good plan will prosper
> in his hands. When he sees all that is
> accomplished by his anguish, he will be
> satisfied. And because of his experience,
> my righteous servant will make it possible
> for many to be counted righteous, for he
> will bear all their sins.
> (NLT Isaiah 53:10-11)

You and I are weak of mind compared to the
Almighty. We find it difficult to understand God's
logic. Could He not have forgiven the sins of true-
believers in another way? Must Jesus have made
the Great Sacrifice? Yes! Our shortcomings in
understanding this matter stem from our poor grasp
of Holiness. Sin is an immense matter in God's
thinking. We trivialize it. Adam could say to
himself, "All I did was eat a piece of fruit." We can
say, "All I did was tell a lie." But, God says that if
You have one unforgiven sin noted in the records
kept in Heaven, You can not enter there. That is
profound. So, God determined that the Great
Sacrifice was essential. He made Jesus the offering
for sin. Jesus' work yielded enormous benefits. He
has many spiritual children in His flock. He will be
satisfied with the results of His suffering.

> Therefore [God says] I will give him a
> portion among the great, and he will divide
> the spoils with the strong, because he
> poured out his life unto death, and was
> numbered with the transgressors. For he

92

bore the sin of many, and made
intercession for the transgressors.
(NIV Isaiah 53:12)

No doubt, Jesus deserves the highest honor among all who have lived. He died for His followers. Here, Isaiah referred to the "strong" spiritual movements that would influence humanity: Christianity, Islam, Buddhism, New-Age Sophistry, and so on. Each of these would claim a segment of mankind, the "spoils" of each belief system. Jesus would get His share of souls and take them to Heaven. Other souls, having been captured by erroneous belief systems, would careen into Hell. Further, Isaiah predicted, Jesus would willingly share Calvary Hill with "transgressors". As He hung there, between the two criminals who would be crucified with Him, He would bear the sins of many. Not all! Looking back at the Cross, through the eyes of the New Testament, we know that Jesus took one of those criminals to Paradise with Himself that very day. (Luke 23:43) He interceded with God the Father, convincing Him to accept His Sacrifice as the payment for that criminal's sins.

Prophecies Highlighted
by New Testament Writers

The passages we have examined predicted many of the details of Jesus' Passion experience. Only a divinely produced Book could contain so many accurate prophecies. In addition to these lengthy passages, many other previews of Jesus' life are found sprinkled throughout the Old Testament. Writers of the New Testament were dedicated to showing how the events of Jesus' life echoed Old

Testament predictions. Let's review some of these events, comparing Mew Testament passages to their antecedents.

- Jesus was born of a virgin. Matthew, an Apostle, noted that an angel of the Lord appeared unto Joseph...

  ...in a dream and said, "Joseph son of David, do not be afraid to take Mary home as your wife, because what is conceived in her is from the Holy Spirit. She will give birth to a son, and you are to give him the name Jesus, because he will save his people from their sins." All this took place to fulfill what the Lord had said through the prophet: "The virgin will conceive and give birth to a son, and they will call him Immanuel" (which means "God with us").
  (NIV Matthew 1:20-23)

  Isaiah had written...

  ...the Lord himself shall give you a sign; Behold, a virgin shall conceive, and bear a son, and shall call his name Immanuel.
  (KJV Isaiah 7:14)

- Jesus was born in Bethlehem...

  ...Joseph...went up from Galilee, out of the city of Nazareth, into Judaea, unto the city of David, which is called Bethlehem; (because he was of the house and lineage of David:) To be taxed

with Mary his espoused wife,
being great with child. And so it
was, that, while they were there,
the days were accomplished that
she should be delivered. And she
brought forth her firstborn son,
and wrapped him in swaddling
clothes, and laid him in a manger;
because there was no room for
them in the inn.
(KJV Luke 2:4-7)

Micah had noted...

...thou, Bethlehem Ephratah,
though thou be little among the
thousands of Judah, yet out of
thee shall he come forth unto me
that is to be ruler in Israel; whose
goings forth have been from of
old, from everlasting.
(KJV Micah 5:2)

Micah mentioned that the child to be born in
Bethlehem, Jesus, had existed "from
everlasting". Of course, Jesus was "in the
beginning" with God. (John 1:1-2)

- Young Jesus was taken to Egypt...
  After the wise men were gone, an
  angel of the Lord appeared to
  Joseph in a dream. "Get up! Flee
  to Egypt with the child and his
  mother," the angel said. "Stay
  there until I tell you to return,
  because Herod is going to search
  for the child to kill him." That
  night Joseph left for Egypt with
  the child and Mary, his mother,

95

and they stayed there until Herod's death. This fulfilled what the Lord had spoken through the prophet: "I called my Son out of Egypt." (NLT Matthew 2:13-15)

Hosea had written down this statement of God...

...out of Egypt I called my son. (NIV Hosea 11:1)

- Herod killed the baby boys of Bethlehem...

    Herod was furious when he realized that the wise men had outwitted him. He sent soldiers to kill all the boys in and around Bethlehem who were two years old and under, based on the wise men's report of the [Nativity] star's first appearance. Herod's brutal action fulfilled what God had spoken through the prophet Jeremiah: "A cry was heard in Ramah — weeping and great mourning. Rachel weeps for her children, refusing to be comforted, for they are dead." (NLT Matthew 2:16-18)

Jeremiah had been told...

    Thus saith the LORD; A voice was heard in Ramah, lamentation, and bitter weeping; Rachel weeping for her children refused to be comforted for her children, because they were not. (KJV Jeremiah 31:15)

- Jesus' ministry was introduced by a prophet...

    ...the word of God came to John son of Zechariah in the wilderness. He went into all the country around the Jordan, preaching a baptism of repentance for the forgiveness of sins. As it is written in the book of the words of Isaiah the prophet: "A voice of one calling in the wilderness, 'Prepare the way for the Lord, make straight paths for him. Every valley shall be filled in, every mountain and hill made low. The crooked roads shall become straight, the rough ways smooth. And all people will see God's salvation.'"
    (NIV Luke 3:2-6)

Isaiah had predicted, there would be...

    A voice of one calling: "In the wilderness prepare the way for the LORD; make straight in the desert a highway for our God. Every valley shall be raised up, every mountain and hill made low; the rough ground shall become level, the rugged places a plain. And the glory of the LORD will be revealed, and all people will see it together. For **the** mouth of the LORD has spoken."
    (NIV Isaiah 40:3-5)

- Jesus did many miracles, such as those described by Matthew, the Apostle...

  > The blind receive their sight, and the lame walk, the lepers are cleansed, and the deaf hear, the dead are raised up, and the poor have the gospel preached to them. (KJV Matthew 11:5)

Isaiah had predicted that when the Messiah would visit Israel, then would...

  > ...the eyes of the blind be opened and the ears of the deaf unstopped. Then will the lame leap like a deer, and the mute tongue shout for joy... (NIV Isaiah 35:5-6)

- On Palm Sunday, Jesus entered Jerusalem upon a donkey...

  > ...they brought the colt to Jesus, and cast their garments on him; and he sat upon him. And many spread their garments in the way: and others cut down branches off the trees, and strawed them in the way. And they that went before, and they that followed, cried, saying, Hosanna; Blessed is he that cometh in the name of the Lord: Blessed be the kingdom of our father David, that cometh in the name of the Lord: Hosanna in the highest. (KJV Mark 11:7-10)

Zechariah had stated...
> Rejoice, O people of Zion! Shout
> in triumph, O people of
> Jerusalem! Look, your king is
> coming to you. He is righteous
> and victorious, yet he is humble,
> riding on a donkey — riding on a
> donkey's colt.
> (NLT Zechariah 9:9)

- Jesus was betrayed by a friend...
  > ...while he [Jesus] yet spake,
  > behold a multitude, and he that
  > was called Judas, one of the
  > twelve, went before them, and
  > drew near unto Jesus to kiss him.
  > (KJV Luke 22:47)

Psalm 41 reads...
> Even my close friend, someone I
> trusted, one who shared my bread,
> has turned against me.
> (NIV Psalm 41:9)

- Jesus was "sold" for 30 pieces of silver...
  > Then one of the Twelve — the
  > one called Judas Iscariot — went
  > to the chief priests and asked,
  > "What are you willing to give me
  > if I deliver him over to you?" So
  > they counted out for him thirty
  > pieces of silver.
  > (NIV Matthew 26:14-15)

Zechariah had been told...
> ...they weighed for my price thirty
> pieces of silver.
> (KJV Zechariah 11:12)

- Jesus was falsely convicted of being a criminal...

> ...with him they crucify two thieves; the one on his right hand, and the other on his left. And the scripture was fulfilled, which saith, And he was numbered with the transgressors.
> (KJV Mark 15:27-28)

Isaiah had said...

> ...he was numbered with the transgressors; and he bare the sin of many, and made intercession for the transgressors.
> (KJV Isaiah 53:12)

- Jesus' hands and feet were pierced. The evening after His Resurrection, Jesus appeared to His Apostles, but Thomas was not there...

> So the other disciples told him, "We have seen the Lord!" But he said to them, "Unless I see the nail marks in his hands and put my finger where the nails were, and put my hand into his side, I will not believe." A week later his disciples were in the house again, and Thomas was with them. Though the doors were locked, Jesus came and stood among them and said, "Peace be with you!" Then he said to Thomas, "Put your finger here; see my hands. Reach out your hand and

put it into my side. Stop doubting
and believe."
(NIV John 20:25-27)
Psalm 22 had long offered this picture of the
Crucifixion...

> ...the assembly of the wicked have
> inclosed me [Jesus]: they pierced
> my hands and my feet.
> (KJV Psalm 22:16)

- A plague of darkness hid the murder of
  Jesus...

> ...from the sixth hour there was
> darkness over all the land unto the
> ninth hour. (KJV Matthew 27:45)

Amos had predicted...

> ...it shall come to pass in that day,
> saith the Lord GOD, that I will
> cause the sun to go down at noon,
> and I will darken the earth in the
> clear day... (KJV Amos 8:9)

- Jesus' bones were not broken...

> ...the soldiers...broke the legs of
> the two men crucified with Jesus.
> But when they came to Jesus,
> they saw that he was already
> dead, so they didn't break his
> legs. One of the soldiers,
> however, pierced his side with a
> spear, and immediately blood and
> water flowed out. (This report is
> from an eyewitness giving an
> accurate account. He speaks the
> truth so that you also can believe.)
> These things happened in

fulfillment of the Scriptures that
say, "Not one of his bones will be
broken..." (NLT John 19:32-36)
Psalm 34 includes these words...
...he [God] protects all his bones,
not one of them will be broken.
(NIV Psalm 34:20)

- On the Cross, Jesus was offered vinegar
  and gall...
  Jesus knew that his mission was
  now finished, and to fulfill
  Scripture he said, "I am thirsty."
  A jar of sour wine was sitting
  there, so they soaked a sponge in
  it, put it on a hyssop branch, and
  held it up to his lips.
  (NLT John 19:28-29)
Psalm 69 reads...
  They put gall in my food and
  gave me vinegar for my thirst.
  (NIV Psalm 69:21)

- Jesus' executioners gambled for His
  clothes...
  When they had crucified him,
  they divided up his clothes by
  casting lots.
  (NIV Matthew 27:35)
Psalm 22 says...
  They divide my clothes among
  them and cast lots for my
  garment. (NIV Psalm 22:18)

- Jesus' side was pierced...

...one of the soldiers pierced
Jesus' side with a spear, bringing
a sudden flow of blood and water.
(NIV John 19:34)

Zechariah, looking past the Cross to the
End-Time, had said...

On that day [when I return to
Earth to defeat the Antichrist and
his armies] I will set out to
destroy all the nations that attack
Jerusalem. And I will pour out on
the house of David and the
inhabitants of Jerusalem a spirit
of grace and supplication. They
will look on me, the one they
have pierced, and they will
mourn...
(NIV Zechariah 12:9-10)

- Jesus was raised from the dead...
    "Don't be alarmed," he [an angel]
    said [to the ladies who had come
    to improve the funeral wrappings
    of Jesus]. "You are looking for
    Jesus the Nazarene, who was
    crucified. He has risen! He is not
    here. See the place where they
    laid him." (NIV Mark 16:6)

Psalm 16 has contained these words of Jesus
for centuries...

...you [Father] will not abandon
me to the realm of the dead, nor
will you let your faithful one see
decay. You make known to me
the path of life; you will fill me
with joy in your presence, with

eternal pleasures at your right
hand. (NIV Psalm 16:10-11)

What a preponderance of evidence! God inspired
the prophets to set down these facts about Jesus for
2 reasons; to convince You and me of the accuracy
of the Bible and to engender an air of expectancy in
the believers of the Old Testament era.

End-Time Prophecies

Both the Old Testament and the New Testament are
replete with predictions about the "End-Time", the
end of the era in which we live. Of course, many of
these prophecies have yet to be fulfilled. I'll
discuss them in more detail in the next chapter.
Here, I'll show You the remarkable, miraculous
nature of the Bible.

One of the most amazing books in the Bible was
written by Daniel. He lived about 6 centuries
before Christ, but God gave him a vision of the end
of our era, known in Bible terms as the "last days".
In the 2600 years since the days of Daniel, some of
his predictions have come to pass, but we are still
looking forward to the fulfillment of the rest of
them.

One of Daniel's prophecies fills me with awe: he
predicted that, someday, the whole earth would
have one ruler, an evil dictator. He noted that this
intensely wicked man would hate God's people and
seek to slay them. What an improbable prediction
this was when he wrote it down. Few have believed
it over the many centuries since his lifetime. But,
now, it seems very plausible. We have the United

Nations which wants to govern the world. We have the World Bank which wants to control the world's monetary systems. Politicians promote the notion of one currency for the whole world. Many of the world's elite want to disarm all the nations, leaving the only military force in the world under the auspices of the UN. World leaders are promoting an international system of taxation to fund these schemes. It is not hard to imagine a crafty politician forming a one-world dictatorship. Daniel saw this coming centuries ago.

For years, skeptics have blown off Daniel's prophecies as a crazy pipe-dream. But, what other book has been in the world's libraries for 26 centuries, predicting such a radical idea? Today, the fulfillment of Daniel's prophecies seems inevitable. Even in America, many of our Presidents, Senators, and Congressmen have embraced the one-world government idea and promoted it diligently.

What did Daniel say? In chapter 7 of his book, in verses 16-27, Daniel wrote the words the Lord delivered to him. He had just seen a vision involving four voracious animals he called "beasts". They quarreled and fought. The fourth beast emerged as the final victor. Daniel himself is one of the characters in his vision. He was confused by what he had seen, so he sought understanding...

> I came near unto one of them [the angels] that stood by, and asked him the truth of all this. So he told me, and made me know the interpretation of the things. These great beasts, which are four, are four kings, which shall arise out of the earth. But the

saints of the most High shall take the
kingdom, and possess the kingdom for
ever, even for ever and ever.
(KJV Daniel 7:16-18)

The angel explained that, from Daniel's time
forward, the world would be dominated by a series
of 4 man-made power structures. But, in the End-
Time, the world would be ruled by the "saints of the
Most High". The word, "saint", is not well
understood today. In the Bible, saints are simply
true-believers. It is comforting to know that true-
believers will "win". Daniel saw it 2600 years ago.
New Testament writers saw it 2000 years ago. The
New Testament affirms that the historic progression
of earthly powers will be succeeded by a Kingdom
ruled by Jesus Christ and the saints of Old and New
Testament times.

Daniel continued...

Then I wanted to know the meaning of the
fourth beast, which was different from all
the others and most terrifying, with its iron
teeth and bronze claws — the beast that
crushed and devoured its victims and
trampled underfoot whatever was left. I
also wanted to know about the ten horns on
its head and about the other horn that came
up, before which three of them fell — the
horn that looked more imposing than the
others and that had eyes and a mouth that
spoke boastfully. (NIV Daniel 7:19-20)

Daniel wanted details of the events shown to him.
So do we. Some of these are explained in the New
Testament. Others, we will not understand until
they transpire. Today, many Bible-believers think
we are in the era of the fourth beast. I do too. This

period began with the formulation of the Roman Empire which has influenced the flow of history for 2 millennia.

Daniel's visions are echoed by John's visions recorded in The Revelation. By combining both sets of visions, we know that the fourth kingdom will morph into 10 divisions, or "horns", at some point in the future. These will vie for power. Then, a mysterious politician will appear on the world's stage, grabbing his power from 3 of the 10 "horns". He will have an awesome appearance and a powerful, oratorical manner of speaking. He will become the dominant figure in world politics. The New Testament prophets called him the "Antichrist".

Daniel continued...

> I beheld, and the same horn made war with
> the saints, and prevailed against them;
> Until the Ancient of days came, and
> judgment was given to the saints of the
> most High; and the time came that the
> saints possessed the kingdom.
> (KJV Daniel 7:21-22)

Daniel's visions did not include all of the events that are prophesied in the New Testament. We will investigate those prophecies in the next chapter, but to put Daniel's visions into a fuller context, I'll sketch these events here. Daniel did not write about the Rapture of the Church. This event will sweep all true-believers off the Earth and into Heaven just before the Antichrist takes control of the world. Immediately thereafter, many of the souls left behind will become Christians in the aftermath of the Rapture. When they see that their godly Mother and all their Christian friends are missing, they will turn to the Bible and to Christ. The Antichrist will hate this. He will make war with these new saints. He will kill most of them and drive the rest into hiding.

Daniel continued...

> ...he [the angel] said, The fourth beast shall be the fourth kingdom upon earth, which shall be diverse from all kingdoms, and shall devour the whole earth, and shall tread it down, and break it in pieces. And the ten horns out of this kingdom are ten kings that shall arise: and another shall rise after them; and he shall be diverse from the first, and he shall subdue three kings. And he shall speak great words against the most High, and shall wear out the saints of the most High, and think to change times and laws: and they shall be given into his hand until a time and times and the dividing of time. (KJV Daniel 7:23-25)

The fourth kingdom, the era since the founding of the Roman Empire, will eventually devolve into 10 kingdoms. Then, the dreadful Antichrist will come to power and subdue 3 of these kingdoms. He will speak "great" words against the "Most High" and seek to destroy any who worship God. He will change the calendar and laws related to holidays. He will not want the Jewish Saturday Sabbath or the Christian Sunday to be observed. He will despise Christmas and Easter. And, he will have his way for "a time", 1 year, and "times", 2 years, and the "dividing of times", a half year. But, after this 3 and 1/2 year period, he will behave like a madman. As we shall see in a later chapter, the New

Testament writers give us additional details about
the Antichrist. He will declare that he himself is
god and require that all mankind worship him.
Then, terrible judgments will befall the whole globe
for 3 and 1/2 years. The Antichrist will try to kill
all who refuse his deification. Many of those who
resist him will flee to Jerusalem. With great rage,
the Antichrist will gather the armies of all nations
and attack the Holy City. He will overthrow it, but
at that point, Jesus will return to Earth to intervene.

Daniel continued...

> But then the court [of Heaven] will pass
> judgment, and all his [the Antichrist's]
> power will be taken away and completely
> destroyed. Then the sovereignty, power,
> and greatness of all the kingdoms under
> heaven will be given to the holy people of
> the Most High. His [Jesus'] kingdom will
> last forever, and all rulers will serve and
> obey him. (NLT Daniel 7:26-27)

Jesus and the saints will take charge of planet Earth.
And, as we shall see in the next chapter, the
Antichrist and his followers will be cast into Hell.
The 1000 year Kingdom described in the New
Testament will dawn.

Yes, Bible-believers have known for 26 centuries
that the political systems of mankind will yield a
one-world government. Their Bibles told them so.
And, for the last 20 centuries, Bible-believers have
known that the wicked, global empire of the
Antichrist will be followed by a wonderful global
Kingdom, under King Jesus. The Lord Himself
taught us to pray for this Kingdom to come. For

centuries, true-believers have prayed, "Thy Kingdom come, Thy will be done in Earth as it is in Heaven." (Matthew 6:10)

So, You see, the Bible is a unique Book. It is accurate. Its Message is cohesive. Each of the 66 books ratifies the others. The Bible presents a logical explanation of the human condition. It is inspiring, because it is written by the One who knows everything; the One who made You and me. And, it is practical. Those who read it and heed it are blessed. I hope You are impressed. Embrace the Holy Book in faith and You will reap profit from it, throughout Eternity.

Boost Five
Jesus Has Created a Reality
Where You May Live
with Him, in Bliss, Forever

What is a reality? It is a period of time and a place in the Universe where a set of natural laws applies. We are living in the "Here and Now". We are accustomed to the way things work in our surroundings. But, the Bible and our Scientists speak of other realities that have existed or will exist or currently exist in parallel with our present reality.

When You were young, You probably stood in the "batter's box" and faced a pitcher who wanted to strike You out. The hurler threw. You swung where You expected the ball to go and missed the ball completely. You thought, "That was a curve! It fooled me." Similarly, our Cosmologists have found that our present reality throws us "curves", at times. They have uncovered features of our present reality that defy "common sense". As You will see, each reality we will discuss is affected by outside forces, objects and beings. For instance, the Bible teaches that God visited "Eden" to walk and talk with Adam and then went elsewhere; that Christ entered our present reality and lived among us for thirty-three years and then went to sit at the right hand of the Father in Heaven. Each reality seems to be nestled inside the ultimate reality that we cannot perceive, presently.

To get a grasp of realities, let's begin by touring a make-believe reality we will call "Flatland". You are point A, and I am point B. Flatland has only 2 dimensions, so no one here has any concept of height, only length and width. As we move along a path, we greet 2 triangles musing about a pair of circles, sitting near the road. Triangles are sharper than the rest of Flatland's citizens, so we listen to their discussion. "Why is this circle normal and that circle stuck?", triangle T asks. Triangle U approaches circle C and finds him to be quite normal. C moves about easily. But, circle D behaves differently. He will not converse with either of the triangles and he is nearly immovable. "I brought a bunch of teenage squares over here, and they struggled to push him a few inches", says triangle T. "Why is he so different from the other circles we know?"

We step back into our "Here and Now" reality, and, immediately, we see the answer to the puzzle facing the triangles. "Circle D" is more than a circle. He is a barrel, full of water, sitting on Flatland. The citizens of Flatland see only the bottom of the barrel, which is a circle. Nature has thrown them a "curve" they cannot comprehend. There is another "dimension" to their reality that they cannot explain. Just so, there are "dimensions" to our "Here and Now" reality that our sharpest thinkers cannot explain.

The ancient Greek geometricians spent a lot of time in a theoretical Flatland. Consider the mathematical constant we call "pi". Long ago, the Greeks took great care to set the value of "pi". It is still very important to us, today, so we owe the Greeks much gratitude. But, generally, their work is misunderstood. If You draw a circle on a sheet of paper and add a straight line passing through its center (a diameter), You are ready to deduce the value of "pi". If You measure the distance around the circle and divide that value by the distance across the circle, You will compute a value close to 3.14, which means that the distance around a circle is slightly more than 3 times the distance across a circle. Because the value of "pi" is so important in the mathematics of physical science, our best thinkers have used laser measuring devices and computers to ascertain the value of "pi" to great accuracy.

By the way, if You wish to demonstrate Your genius to some friends, memorize this phrase: "See, I have a rhyme assisting my feeble brain its tasks ofttimes resisting." Now, if You recite this sentence to Yourself and count the letters in each word and speak them out, You will state the value of "pi" quite precisely, 3.141592653589. But, even that is not quite the true value. Mathematicians have proved that no one can ever state the value exactly. The decimal values of "pi" proceed endlessly.

As an example of the "curves" that our reality throws at us, let's consider one that our mariners discovered years ago. The Earth is not flat. If the Greeks had made their circles on the ground and made them very large, the values they calculated for "pi" would have been less than "pi". Think of it this way; if they had made a circle at the Equator and drawn its diameter through the North Pole, they would have set the value of "pi" at about 2. That's because the diameter crossing the North Pole **would** reach 1/2 way around the Earth and the circle at the Equator would reach all the way around the Earth. So, what is true on a flat sheet of paper is not true on the spherical surface of the Earth in our "Here and Now" reality.

And, here is another "curve". If You look at a map of the United States, You will see that Sacramento, California is about due West of Raleigh, North Carolina. If You strike a straight line between the cities, You may think that this line represents the most direct flight path from one of the cities to the other. However, because we live on a spherical planet, that is not true. Mathematicians tell us that the shortest path between 2 points on a sphere is an "arc of a great circle". A "great circle" is a circle drawn on the surface of the Earth that has as its midpoint the center of the Earth. The Equator is a good example. Now, pretend You have a "hula hoop" the size of the Equator. If You position it so that it is snug to the Earth and has its rim passing through Raleigh and Sacramento, You will notice that the rim of the hoop bows up toward Chicago. If You travel the path traced by the rim, You will fly less miles than You will if You fly due West. Quirky, but true.

Early last century, Albert Einstein, pointed out other quirks in our "Here and Now" reality. He noted experimental data from many physical phenomena and proposed a theory of "Relativity" that rocked the scientific community. And, as his ideas were subjected to rigorous tests, they proved to be true.

Einstein's most debated conclusion was that the speed at which light travels is essentially constant, about 186,000 miles per second and that nothing in our space-time reality can travel faster than light-speed. People argued, "This does not square with reality." They reasoned that if You were driving toward me with Your speedometer reading 60 miles per hour, and I were driving toward You with my speedometer reading 60 miles per hour, then we would perceive that we were approaching each other at 120 miles per hour. So, they presumed that if You were in a spaceship approaching me at 90% of the speed of light, and I were in a spaceship traveling toward You at 90% of the speed of light, that the speed at which we were approaching one another would be 180% of light-speed. Einstein said, "No, your relative speed cannot exceed light-speed." He introduced changes in the prevailing laws of motion that reduced the relative speed that we calculated, 180% of light-speed, to less than the speed of light. Using his equations in the case of the cars, the approach speed would be slightly less than 120 miles per hour. Not much. Just a minuscule amount. But, in the case of the spaceships, his equations predict a much lower approach speed than we assumed.

Even more bizarre were other predictions based on Einstein's theory of Relativity:

- Time passes more slowly at the bottom of a mountain than at the top, because of gravitational forces.
- When traveling between two planets, the faster you travel, the shorter the distance traveled becomes.
- The faster you travel, the slower time passes, so when an astronaut returns to Earth after traveling near the speed of

light for several years, he would have aged less than those who stayed on Earth.

Of great interest to Bible-believers are Einstein's notions about gravity. No one really knows how gravity works. It is as mysterious to us as the heavy circle was to the inhabitants of Flatland. Einstein set the Cosmologists of our world on a great search for a better understanding of gravity. We can do a crude experiment to illustrate Einstein's ideas. Let's go outside to Your trampoline. You get on one side. I'll take the other. Now, roll a baseball to me. See, it follows a straight path across the canvas. Now, let's place a very heavy, steel ball in the middle of Your trampoline and try the same thing. See, the baseball no longer travels in a straight line. It "falls" inward, toward the steel ball. In a similar way, gravity puts a curve in our space-time reality. Einstein proposed that space is a kind of fabric. Each object in space makes a "dent" in the fabric, so other objects "fall" toward it. Now, our experiment is crude, because it only deals with a flat canvas fabric. In reality, the fabric of space is three-dimensional and acts in every direction.

This notion of a cosmic fabric has been expanded by many Cosmologists over the last century. The consensus today is that everything in the Universe is made of extremely tiny "strings". Even sub-atomic particles like electrons are clusters of tiny strings. The whole Universe is a fabric of strings, knit together in countless ways. This thinking excites Christians, because, without knowing a thing about the theory of strings, Bible authors, long ago, spoke prophetically of the fabric of the Universe.

116

Consider these Scripture passages and be amazed. They liken our Universe to the fabrics of "scrolls" and "clothes" and "garments"...

- All the stars in the sky will be dissolved and the heavens rolled up like a scroll; all the starry host will fall like withered leaves from the vine, like shriveled figs from the fig tree. (NIV Isaiah 34:4)
- Lift up your eyes to the heavens, and look upon the earth beneath: for the heavens shall vanish away like smoke, and the earth shall wax old [grow old] like a garment...
  (KJV Isaiah 51:6)
- In the beginning, Lord, you laid the foundation of the earth and made the heavens with your hands. They will perish, but you remain forever. They will wear out like old clothing. You will fold them up like a cloak and discard them like old clothing. (NLT Hebrews 1:10-12)
- ...the stars in the sky fell to earth, as figs drop from a fig tree when shaken by a strong wind. The heavens receded like a scroll being rolled up, and every mountain and island was removed from its place.
  (NIV The Revelation 6:13-14)

This convergence of thoughts from the ancient men of God and the modern physicists is remarkable.

The Many Realities of Man

From the Bible, we know of at least 9 realities. These are listed and discussed below. We will see that every man or woman ever born is still alive. Each of us is forever. When we die, we will move on to another reality. Christians eagerly look forward to a sequence of exciting, future realities. Let's explore the realities of the past, present, and future.

As You share the following list of realities with others, You will note that Christians do not agree, unanimously, with this list. Nor do they all agree with the descriptions of these realities as I have given them, here. That is refreshing, since Christians should vigorously study the Scriptures and debate the meaning of each verse. It can be great fun. But, be assured, after You hear the debates, that all Christians look forward to a thrilling future with Christ. That is why You will hear Bible students say, "I have read the end of the Book. We win!"

1. The "Eden" Reality

Adam and Eve lived in a beautiful garden. They spoke with the Lord each day. There was no death in their reality. All the animals were vegetarians. It is awesome to imagine them playing with lions, eating berries off a bush while standing next to a bear, or swimming with alligators. There was no rain in the Garden of Eden. Much of the water on Earth was underground. Each morning, a mist would emanate from the soil to water the plants. This Paradise was ruined by sin. God had given one rule to Adam and Eve...

> ...of the tree of the knowledge of good and evil, thou shalt not eat...for in the day that thou eatest thereof thou shalt surely die. (KJV Genesis 2:17)

When our first parents broke this rule, they were evicted from this reality.

2. The "Pre-Flood" Reality

As Adam left Eden, God put a curse on His Creation. He informed Adam...

> ... Cursed is the ground because of you;
> through painful toil you will eat food from
> it all the days of your life. It will produce
> thorns and thistles for you, and you will eat
> the plants of the field. By the sweat of your
> brow you will eat your food until you
> return to the ground, since from it you
> were taken; for dust you are and to dust
> you will return. (NIV Genesis 3:17-19)

This "Pre-Flood" reality was quite different from "Eden". Still, there was no rain. A daily mist watered the Earth. But, death was everywhere. Animals ate other animals. Even man ate meat. Still, the air, the water and the food were much better than that which we have today. People lived for hundreds of years. This reality persisted until the world-wide Flood of Noah's day. Just as sin had brought an end to the "Eden" reality, rampant sin brought an end to this reality. God said unto Noah...

> ...I am going to put an end to all people, for
> the earth is filled with violence because of
> them. I am surely going to destroy both
> them and the earth. (NIV Genesis 6:13)

All but the eight souls on the ark were killed by the Flood.

3. The "Pre–Babel" Reality

This reality commenced when Noah's ark landed on
Mount Ararat. Things were much different. No
longer did the morning mist water the Earth. The
underground water system had been broken up.
The seas were much larger. God installed a new
system of evaporation and condensation to produce
rain. Just as it is today, vast weather systems began
to move across the continents. In this reality, life-
spans became much shorter. Again, sinful pleasures
became the primary motivator of the citizens. Sin
expressed itself in a defiant pride. The people
said...

> [Let us]...build...a city and a tower, whose
> top may reach unto heaven; and let us
> make us a name... (KJV Genesis 11:4)

Apparently, their pride carried them to the extreme.
They imagined that they were gods. Instead of
worshiping the true God, they worshiped
themselves. God would have none of it. He said...

> ...let us...confound their language, that they
> may not understand one another's speech.
> So the LORD scattered them abroad from
> thence upon the face of all the earth...
> (KJV Genesis 11:7-8)

Some Christians believe the curse of Babel went
beyond vocabulary, involving the very organs of
speech production. If so, the physical differences
may not have shown up at the moment the curse
was pronounced. They may have appeared in the
future offspring of the diverse groups that were
created by the curse. Some of the dispersed tribes
had square jaws, others oval faces. Some, thin lips,
others thick. Some, large vocal boxes, others small.

We do not know the "depth" of the curse, but we do know that the purpose of the curse was to make the tribes "strange" to each other. Prejudices began to cause the groups to disassociate. Great migrations occurred. People clustered with those most like themselves.

4. The "Here and Now" Reality

From the days of the Tower of Babel till today, our present reality has been in place. The peoples of the Earth are still divided by language barriers and physical differences. Large weather systems still sweep across the continents, bringing blessings and mayhem. The immense oceans still hold the remnants of Noah's Flood. Men and women, still, must sweat to garner their daily bread. The diversities derived from Babel continually plague the planet. Wars and rumors of wars are endemic. The various tribes still mistrust those who are different. But, praise God, during this reality, Christ appeared and He gave us a profound hope of better realities to come.

As we have discussed, our present reality has its mysterious "curves". Our best thinkers are diligently trying to unravel these baffling forces and components of our time period. Someday, those of us who are saved, will rise above this reality and see what is behind these "curves".

During this era, we have received many visitors from Heaven. Moses met God on Mount Sinai. Daniel talked with angels. Jesus became a man and lived among us. But, for most of us modern earthlings, God seems to be veiled. We Christians feel His presence when we pray and worship, but we eagerly look forward to future realities where the Father, Son and Holy Spirit will be wonderfully accessible to us.

At the end of this "Here and Now" reality, an epoch the Bible calls the "Day of the Lord" begins. This period over-arches three realities. Its first 7 years are the last 7 years of the "Here and Now" reality. Its next 1000 years span the entire "Millennium" reality. And, its last days are the first days of the "New Heaven and Earth" reality. Interestingly, we who live in the present reality do not know when this epoch will begin. The Apostle Peter said...

>...the day of the Lord will come as a thief in the night... (KJV II Peter 3:10)

Jesus said...

>...no one knows the day or hour when these things will happen, not even the angels in heaven or the Son himself. Only the Father knows. When the Son of Man returns, it will be like it was in Noah's day. In those days before the flood, the people were enjoying banquets and parties and weddings right up to the time Noah entered his boat. People didn't realize what was going to happen until the flood came and swept them all away. That is the way it will be when the Son of Man comes. (NLT Matthew 24:36-39)

God has not revealed, to us, when the "Day of the Lord" will begin. He has left the timing "iffy", to keep Christians ever vigilant. He wants us to live as though the "Day of the Lord" could start at any time. Even though the folks in Noah's day were warned by Noah of the impending flood, even though they saw the completion of the ark, even though they saw the in-gathering of the animals, as they boarded ship, still, they refused to believe. Just so, after thousands of years filled with persistent warnings voiced by true-believers, most of mankind refuses to believe the Bible's Message. These unbelievers will be caught off-guard when the "Day of the Lord" starts and Jesus comes to Earth again.

The first event of the "Day of the Lord" is called the "Rapture". This is not a Bible word, but we Christians use the term, because it describes how we will feel when this exciting event occurs. Unexpectedly, Jesus will return to Earth. and He will sweep all true-believers off the planet. The Apostle Paul wrote...

> ...we believe that Jesus died and was raised to life again, we also believe that when Jesus returns, God will bring back with him the believers who have died. We tell you this directly from the Lord: We who are still living when the Lord returns will not meet him ahead of those who have died. For the Lord himself will come down from heaven with a commanding shout, with the voice of the archangel, and with the trumpet call of God. First, the Christians who have died will rise from their graves. Then, together with them, we who are still alive and remain on the earth will be caught up in the clouds to meet the Lord in the air. Then we will be with the Lord forever. So encourage each other with these words.
> (NLT I Thessalonians 4:14-18)

Did You grasp the details? The deceased saved of all ages are currently in a "Pre-Millennium Heaven", described below. They will appear with Jesus in the clouds. Then, Jesus will call their bodies from their graves to be united with their heavenly bodies. Why? Well, when Jesus was resurrected, He did not leave His earthly body in the tomb. His body was revived and transformed into His Heavenly body. Also, the Christians alive at the moment of the Rapture will take their transformed bodies with them to meet the Lord. So, it seems fitting that those believers now dwelling in the "Pre-Millennium Heaven" should be re-united with their earthly bodies.

What a shocking time this will be. All true-believers will rise to meet Christ in the sky. You have probably heard Christians sing, "I'll Fly Away". Indeed, they will. The Apostle Paul added this information...

> ...let me reveal to you a wonderful secret. We will not all die, but we will all be transformed! It will happen in a moment, in the blink of an eye, when the last trumpet is blown. For when the trumpet sounds, those who have died will be raised to live forever. And we who are living will also be transformed. For our dying bodies must be transformed into bodies that will never die; our mortal bodies must be transformed into immortal bodies.
> (NLT I Corinthians 15:51-53)

Can You imagine the global upset when, suddenly, all the Christians are gone. The best Church congregations will be left with no members. Of

124

course, some "phony churches" will continue their normal activities, for they were never really Christians. But, who will explain all the "missing persons"? If You are not a Christian when this Rapture occurs, all Your believing friends will be nowhere to be found. You and others that are "left behind" will give very serious consideration to the Bible. And, fortunately, many will come to faith through this astounding event.

Christians refer to the first 7 years of the "Day of the Lord" as "The Tribulation", because this period will witness world-wide catastrophes. In one of his letters to the Church at Thessalonica, the Apostle Paul gave this sequence of events: first, the Church will be "stolen" off the Earth by Jesus Christ, as if by a "thief in the night". Next, a season of "peace and safety" will ensue. Finally, the Tribulation period will end in "sudden destruction" under the wrath of God. Paul wrote...

> ...you know very well that the day of the Lord will come like a thief in the night. While people are saying, "Peace and safety," destruction will come on them suddenly, as labor pains on a pregnant woman, and they will not escape. But you, brothers and sisters, are not in darkness so that this day should surprise you like a thief. You are all children of the light and children of the day. We do not belong to the night or to the darkness. So then, let us not be like others, who are asleep, but let us be awake and sober. For those who sleep, sleep at night, and those who get drunk, get drunk at night. But since we belong to the day, let us be sober, putting

on faith and love as a breastplate, and the hope of salvation as a helmet. For God did not appoint us to suffer wrath but to receive salvation through our Lord Jesus Christ. He died for us so that, whether we are awake or asleep, we may live together with him. Therefore encourage one another and build each other up, just as in fact you are doing. (NIV I Thessalonians 5:2-11)

As Paul said, we Christians, who are the "children of the light", do not need to fear this period. "God did not appoint us to suffer wrath." Whether we are "awake", are alive, or "sleep", are deceased, when the Rapture occurs and the Tribulation begins, we will live out this era "together" with Jesus.

The Tribulation will be dominated by a charismatic, ruthless man known to Bible students as the "Antichrist". This era will be divided into 2 equal parts. During the first half of the period, the Antichrist will lead all the nations of the world into a one-world government. He will become the dictator of all mankind. At first, he will seem to be successful. A tentative peace will be put in place. But, new converts to Christianity will irritate him. In fact, all religions will provoke him. He will allow the Jews to rebuild their Temple in Jerusalem and re-institute their sacrifice system. He will try to be friends with Muslims, Hindus, and every other sect in the world. But, after 3 and 1/2 years, with the urgings of Satan, he will decide to eradicate all existing religions and will insist that every man, woman and child worship him. He will step into the Jewish Temple in Jerusalem and declare, "I am god. Worship me!" In the words of the Apostle Paul, the Antichrist...

...will exalt himself and defy everything
that people call god and every object of
worship. He will even sit in the temple of
God, claiming that he himself is God.
(NLT II Thessalonians 2:4)

The next 3 and 1/2 years will be filled with
catastrophes. The period will be reminiscent of the
time when Judgment after Judgment fell on Egypt
before the Pharaoh capitulated and let Israel go.
The calamities, disease, and mayhem of this time
are described in the pages of the last book of the
Bible, The Revelation. The Antichrist, with Satan's
goading, will become a madman, seeking to murder
everyone who refuses to deny Jesus and worship
him.

Most of the individuals who will become Christians,
in the wake of the Rapture and the appearance of
the Antichrist, will be martyred. The Apostle John,
in the Revelation, calls the Antichrist "the beast",
and tells us of this edict that the Antichrist will
institute...
> ...as many as would not worship the image
> of the beast should be killed.
> (KJV The Revelation 13:15)

Many Jews and Christians will take refuge in
Jerusalem. The Antichrist will react violently. He
will lead the armies of the world against the Holy
City. In his prophetic vision, the Apostle John saw
3 evil spirits. He said...
> ...they are the spirits of devils, working
> miracles, which go forth unto the kings of
> the earth and of the whole world, to gather

them to the battle of that great day of God
Almighty. (KJV The Revelation 16:14)
This international army will join the Antichrist for
the attack on Jerusalem. In the Revelation, John
noted that the Antichrist...

> ...gathered them together into a place
> called in the Hebrew tongue Armageddon.
> (KJV The Revelation 16:16)

Centuries ago, Zechariah saw this army sacking
Jerusalem. And, he saw Christ returning from
Heaven to intervene...

> Watch, for the day of the LORD is coming
> when your possessions will be plundered
> right in front of you! I will gather all the
> nations to fight against Jerusalem. The city
> will be taken, the houses looted, and the
> women raped...Then the LORD will go out
> to fight against those nations, as he has
> fought in times past.
> (NLT Zechariah 14:1-3)

Christ will annihilate the Antichrist and the heathen
armies in the valley of Armageddon. In his
Revelation, John saw Jesus, seated on a white horse,
leading the charge...

> ...I saw the beast [the Antichrist], and the
> kings of the earth, and their armies,
> gathered together to make war against him
> that sat on the horse, and against his army.
> And the beast was taken...[and] cast alive
> into a lake of fire burning with brimstone.
> And the remnant were slain...
> (KJV The Revelation 19:19-21)

The Antichrist and his entourage will be consigned
to Hell.

Once again, great sin will mark the end of a reality. Jesus will begin His reign over planet Earth and all mankind. The "Day of the Lord" will continue in the "Millennium" reality, discussed below.

5. The "Paradise" Reality

From the "Pre-Flood" era to, approximately, the moment when Jesus ascended into Heaven to sit at the right hand of the Father, "Paradise" existed as a parallel reality to the others we have catalogued here. It may still exist, but most Christians believe Jesus took its inhabitants to Heaven with Him when He returned there. (Psalm 68:18 and Ephesians 4:8) Its first resident was, probably, righteous Abel, after he was murdered by Cain. From thence, it became the home of all who died as true-believers, until Jesus led its citizens to "Pre-Millennium Heaven", discussed below.

Jesus spoke of Paradise. He told of 2 men who had died, a rich man and a beggar. (Luke 16:20-31) The rich man went to Hell. The poor man went to "Abraham's Bosom", another name for Paradise. The rich man could see Abraham and the former beggar afar off. He could communicate with them, but he could not approach them, because Hell and Paradise were separated by a "great gulf". Even so, it is interesting to note that Hell and Paradise were within sight of one another.

As Jesus suffered on His Cross, one of the criminals who was executed with Him became a believer. He claimed Jesus as his Lord...

Jesus answered him, "Truly I tell you,
today you will be with me in paradise."
(NIV Luke 23:43)

"Paradise" was, probably, like the Garden of Eden
and served as a pleasant resting place for those Old
Testament saints who were awaiting the
Incarnation, Ministry, Sacrifice, Resurrection and
Ascension of Christ.

6. The "Pre-Millennium Heaven" Reality

Since Jesus' return to Heaven, all true-believers go
to be with Him in "Pre-Millennium Heaven" when
they die. The Apostle Paul wrote...

...we are always confident, even though we
know that as long as we live in these
bodies we are not at home with the Lord.
For we live by believing and not by seeing.
Yes, we are fully confident, and we would
rather be away from these earthly bodies,
for then we will be at home with the Lord.
(NLT II Corinthians 5:6-8)

And, when we see Him, we will be transformed.
Our new bodies will be amazing. The Apostle John
wrote...

Dear friends, now we are children of God,
and what we will be has not yet been made
known. But we know that when Christ
appears, we shall be like him, for we shall
see him as he is. (NIV I John 3:2)

The "Pre-Millennium Heaven" reality is like a
festive reunion where the Family of God awaits the
future realities our Father has scheduled. Old

Testament saints such as Moses and Abraham and David are there. New Testament saints such as Peter and Paul and John are there, now. Perhaps, Your parents are there, watching and waiting for You, praying that You will choose to join them. All the residents of this reality are eager to see the "Day of the Lord" and the start of the "Millennium" reality.

7. The "Hell" Reality

This is the infamous, very negative reality that has existed in parallel with the other realities mentioned here. But, unlike "Paradise", "Hell" is still a very busy place and will remain so forever. Christ often spoke of "Hell". In Matthew 22:13, He called it "outer darkness", a place where there is "weeping and gnashing of teeth." In Matthew 23:33, He called it a place of "damnation". In Mark 9:43, He referred to it as a place where there is a "fire that never shall be quenched", and He described the body of a person who goes there as a "worm" that "dieth not". In Luke 16:34, He depicted a resident of "Hell" as "being in torments". Contrary to the thinking of some, Hell is not a "honky-tonk" where bad boys and girls fritter away Eternity. It is terrifying to contemplate living in Hell, yet, most of the human race is headed there. Jesus taught...

Enter [Heaven] through the narrow gate. For wide is the gate and broad is the road that leads to destruction [Hell], and many enter through it. But small is the gate and narrow the road that leads to life, and only a few find it. (NIV Matthew 7:13-14)

131

8. The "Millennium" Reality

For centuries Christians have prayed, "...thy kingdom come, thy will be done on Earth...". In so doing, we have been praying for the "Millennium" reality, when Jesus returns to Earth and reigns for a thousand years. The details of this era are given in The Revelation, chapter 20. At the onset of the period, Satan will be bound and jailed in a bottomless pit until the last days of that era. When he is freed, Satan will lead a rebellion against King Jesus. Of course, he will lose, and he will be cast into the region of Hell known as the "Lake of Fire", never to trouble mankind again.

As mentioned earlier, the "Day of the Lord" will begin 7 years before the end of the "Here and Now" reality. It will continue throughout the entire "Millennium" reality and end at the onset of the "New Heaven and Earth" reality.

Who will live during this "Millennium" period? Christians speculate. For sure, the saints who have been waiting in "Pre-Millennium Heaven" for this reality to dawn. And, any souls on Earth who have survived "The Tribulation", which will close-out the "Here and Now" reality. This group will include both saved believers and unsaved non-believers. Further, some Christians believe that the "innocents" who died in former realities will be resurrected to live in this reality, having their chance to choose Jesus as their Savior. This group would include aborted babies, persons born without comprehension, and, possibly, those who never heard of Jesus during their lifetimes.

King Jesus will rule. He taught His disciples...

> ...I assure you that when the world is made
> new and the Son of Man sits upon his
> glorious throne, you who have been my
> followers will also sit on twelve thrones,
> judging the twelve tribes of Israel.
> (NLT Matthew 19:28)

Won't it be glorious to see the planet "made new",
looking as it did when Adam first opened his eyes?

Isaiah was given a thrilling picture of this reality.
Speaking of the citizens of the "Millennium", he
wrote...

> ...they shall beat their swords into
> plowshares, and their spears into
> pruninghooks: nation shall not lift up
> sword against nation, neither shall they
> learn war any more. (KJV Isaiah 2:4)

and...

> In that day the wolf and the lamb will live
> together; the leopard will lie down with the
> baby goat. The calf and the yearling will
> be safe with the lion, and a little child will
> lead them all. The cow will graze near the
> bear. The cub and the calf will lie down
> together. The lion will eat hay like a cow.
> The baby will play safely near the hole of a
> cobra. Yes, a little child will put its hand in
> a nest of deadly snakes without harm.
> Nothing will hurt or destroy in all my holy
> mountain, for as the waters fill the sea, so
> the earth will be filled with people who
> know the LORD. (NLT Isaiah 11:6-9)

Eden will be restored. The underground irrigation
system will once again water the plants. All

creatures will again be vegetarians. Plants will produce bountiful, delicious fruits.

Jesus will set His throne in Jerusalem. Then, the Apostles will be seated. In The Revelation, the Apostle John wrote...

> ...I saw thrones, and they sat upon them, and judgment was given unto them: and I saw the souls of them that were beheaded for the witness of Jesus, and for the word of God, and which had not worshipped the beast [the Antichrist], neither his image, neither had received his mark upon their foreheads, or in their hands; and they lived and reigned with Christ a thousand years. But the rest of the dead lived not again until the thousand years were finished. This is the first resurrection. Blessed and holy is he that hath part in the first resurrection: on such the second death hath no power, but they shall be priests of God and of Christ, and shall reign with him a thousand years.
> (KJV The Revelation 20:4-6)

It is imperative that You resolve to be in "the first resurrection". It will be exhilarating. To be included in this spectacular event, You must be "born again", as we have discussed earlier. Those who are born twice, physically and spiritually, die only once, physically. But, those who are born only once, who never experience the second spiritual birth, will die a "second death" when they are cast into Hell. The wages, the pay-off, for harboring unforgiven sins will be the "second death".

134

John separated those who will "reign" with Christ during the "Millennium" into 3 groups: those who were beheaded for their testimony about Jesus, those who were beheaded for believing the Word of God, and those who had not worshiped the Antichrist. This latter group will be huge. The spirit of Antichrist has been around throughout human history. When one opposes the way of the world, he or she is refusing to worship the Antichrist. True-believers have consistently rejected the marks of worldliness. Sure, there will be those who will have to confront the evil Antichrist face to face, but he has been opposed, in spirit, by believers of every era.

Because Christians hold diverse opinions about the makeup of the "Millennium" population, I offer, here, my speculations, in order to highlight issues that are debated among the saved. Only God knows the whole truth. Certainly, the "resurrected saints", all of us who have trusted in Jesus, will inhabit this reality. I do not believe that we will be male or female in our resurrected forms. Hence, we will not procreate. Jesus said...

> ...The children of this world marry, and are given in marriage: But they which shall be accounted worthy to obtain that world, and the resurrection from the dead, neither marry, nor are given in marriage: Neither can they die any more: for they are equal unto the angels; and are the children of God, being the children of the resurrection. (KJV Luke 20:34-36)

Even though the resurrected saints will not have any children in this era, the quotations from Isaiah, given above, indicate that there will be little ones present. These are the offspring of the ordinary humans who survive the 7 year Tribulation period at the end of the "Here and Now" reality. And, as we mentioned earlier, it may be that the innocents of prior realities are given a new life and a chance to make Jesus their King. This would add many souls to the population. Also, note that in chapter 65 of his book, Isaiah speaks of some of the "Millennium" citizens dying of old age. That cannot be any of the resurrected saints, for Jesus said, "Neither can they die any more." Further, at the end of this reality, many citizens rebel against King Jesus and die in the ensuing battle. Certainly, none of these rebels will be resurrected saints. So, we must conclude that the Earth is inhabited by an interesting mixture: King Jesus, resurrected saints, and ordinary human beings.

Those who believe that the innocents will be given a second life, during the "Millennium", point out that this would be proper. They reason: If a resurrected innocent chooses to be a follower of Jesus, he or she will move on, ultimately, to the next Heavenly reality, the "New Heaven and Earth". But, if an innocent rejects Jesus, he or she will end up in Hell. This arrangement would assure that every citizen of the "New Heaven and Earth" freely chose Jesus as his or her King.

Many of the ordinary humans of the "Millennium" era will become Christians under the tutelage of Jesus and His resurrected saints, who are called "priests of God", because they will endeavor to lead the unsaved of the "Millennium" into saving faith. But, staggering as it is, even after meeting King

Jesus and fraternizing with His impressive cadre of priests and enjoying the glory of the "Millennium" paradise, some will refuse to acknowledge the authority of Christ, the Father, and the Holy Spirit. They will join Satan in a rebellion against the Lord. How can this be? Well, remember, Satan and all the evil spirits were once angels in Heaven, in the presence of the Trinity, and they refused to have the Godhead reign over them.

As we have noted, at the end of the "Millennium", Satan is freed and is allowed to woo the citizens of the era into rebellion against Jesus and the priests...

> ...Satan will be let out of his prison. He will go out to deceive the nations — called Gog and Magog — in every corner of the earth. He will gather them together for battle — a mighty army, as numberless as sand along the seashore. And I saw them as they went up on the broad plain of the earth and surrounded God's people and the beloved city. But fire from heaven came down on the attacking armies and consumed them. Then the devil, who had deceived them, was thrown into the fiery lake of burning sulfur, joining the beast and the false prophet. There they will be tormented day and night forever and ever. (NLT The Revelation 20:7-10)

After this defeat, Satan will never again be a problem for mankind. Only the saved will be alive on the Earth. The moment for the final Judgment will arrive. John provided an eye-witness testimony to that event...

...I saw a great white throne, and him that sat on it, from whose face the earth and the heaven fled away; and there was found no place for them. And I saw the dead, small and great, stand before God; and the books were opened: and another book was opened, which is the book of life: and the dead were judged out of those things which were written in the books, according to their works. And the sea gave up the dead which were in it; and death and hell delivered up the dead which were in them: and they were judged every man according to their works. And death and hell were cast into the lake of fire. This is the second death. And whosoever was not found written in the book of life was cast into the lake of fire. (KJV The Revelation 20:11-15)

Did You know that the events of Your life are being recorded? John said that all your works and thoughts are being recorded in "books" that will be opened on Judgment Day. Now, remember that just one unforgiven sin will send You to Hell. This is frightening, until You study the Bible and realize that every transgression You have ever committed, every nasty thought You have ever had can be blotted out of those "books" by the Sacrificial Blood Jesus shed on the Cross. In the book of Acts, Luke recorded words the Apostle Peter preached in Jerusalem. Peter asked his listeners to consider...

...those things, which God before [in the Old Testament Scriptures] had shewed [revealed] by the mouth of all his prophets, that Christ should suffer, he hath so fulfilled. Repent ye therefore, and be converted, that your sins may be blotted out, when the times of refreshing shall come from the presence of the Lord. And

he shall send Jesus Christ, which before
was preached unto you: Whom the heaven
must receive until the times of restitution
of all things, which God hath spoken by
the mouth of all his holy prophets since the
world began. (KJV Acts 3:18-21)

How exciting! Peter asked his hearers (and that
includes You and me) to repent and be converted so
that our sins will be blotted out of those "books"
that are to be used on Judgment Day. Now, if all
Your sins are blotted out of those "books", and,
then, You are judged only by what remains, only
the good things You have done will be used to
judge You. Hallelujah, praise God! There will be
nothing in those "books" to condemn You!

The epic battle between Good and Evil will be over.
All the beings who have opposed Almighty God
will have been defeated and condemned to Hell
forever. The "Day of the Lord" will continue into
the next reality.

9. The "New Heaven and Earth" Reality

What happens after the "Millennium"? As we
documented earlier, all the unsaved humans, Satan,
and all his evil spirits will be consigned to their
eternal punishments at the end of that thousand year
reality.

In his second epistle, the Apostle Peter said a final
reality will dawn at this future moment...

...the day of the Lord will come as
unexpectedly as a thief. Then the heavens
will pass away with a terrible noise, and
the very elements themselves will

disappear in fire, and the earth and everything on it will be found to deserve judgment. Since everything around us is going to be destroyed like this, what holy and godly lives you should live, looking forward to the day of God and hurrying it along. On that day, he will set the heavens on fire, and the elements will melt away in the flames. But we are looking forward to the new heavens and new earth he has promised, a world filled with God's righteousness. (NLT II Peter 3:10-13)

We noted earlier that at the onset of the "Millennium", the Earth and its atmosphere will be "regenerated". The whole of nature will become like that Adam and Eve enjoyed in the Garden of Eden. Even though this paradise will seem, to the saved, to be a fine place in which to dwell for all Eternity, God has an even more impressive "ultimate" reality planned for His saints. The "Millennium" Earth will bear the scars of the last battle with Satan and his band of rebels. Perhaps, there will still be other reminders of the long, vicious history of the planet, such as the "swords that will be beaten into plowshares." (Isaiah 2:4) Whatever His reasons, God, in His infinite wisdom, has decided to incinerate Earth and replace it with a "New Heaven and Earth".

Did You note, here, that Peter called the "Day of the Lord" the "Day of God"? He said You and I should be "looking forward to the day of God...On that day, he will set the heavens on fire, and the elements will melt away in the flames." Give Yourself to Jesus, and You will eagerly anticipate this future event, for it heralds the start of the "New Heaven and Earth" reality.

This dramatic inferno will be the climax of the "Day of the Lord". With great noise, the very elements that make up the material world will melt. The Earth and the structures men have built upon it will be burned. The whole of the "Millennium" reality will be dissolved. So, Peter encouraged us to look forward to the "New Heaven and Earth" reality, which will be filled with righteousness. Jesus taught...

> Blessed are they which do hunger and
> thirst after righteousness: for they shall be
> filled. (KJV Matthew 5:6)

This promise will be fulfilled in the "New Heaven and Earth" reality.

The Apostle John, in his recording of The Revelation, gave us more details...

> ...I saw a new heaven and a new earth: for
> the first heaven and the first earth were
> passed away; and there was no more sea.
> (KJV The Revelation 21:1)

Since the Great Flood of Noah's day, the seas have covered a large portion of the Earth, but John noticed that the seas will not be a part of the New Earth.

> ...I John saw the holy city, new Jerusalem,
> coming down from God out of heaven,
> prepared as a bride adorned for her
> husband. (KJV The Revelation 21:2)

Often, the Bible refers to the whole body of true-believers of all time as the "Bride of Christ". Carrying that terminology further, the Bible says that the Bride of Christ, the Church, will be united with Christ at the "marriage of the Lamb" (The Revelation 19:7), up in Heaven. In harmony with that festive occasion, the New Jerusalem will also be decked out as a bride, in gleaming white, adorned with precious jewels.

> And I heard a great voice out of heaven saying, Behold, the tabernacle of God is with men, and he will dwell with them, and they shall be his people, and God himself shall be with them, and be their God.
> (KJV The Revelation 21:3)

This event will mark a huge departure from the nature of all the previous realities. God will place His Tabernacle and His Throne in the midst of the saved of mankind. The "veil" that has hidden God from man in most of the previous realities will be gone. The redeemed will see God's full splendor and be able to approach the Father, the Son, and the Holy Spirit, freely.

> And God shall wipe away all tears from their eyes; and there shall be no more death, neither sorrow, nor crying, neither shall there be any more pain: for the former things are passed away.
> (KJV The Revelation 21:4)

The curse that chased Adam and Eve from Eden and weighed on mankind through so many eras will be fully and permanently removed.

> And he that sat upon the throne said, Behold, I make all things new. And he said unto me, Write: for these words are true and faithful. (KJV The Revelation 21:5)

Everything will be new. There will be nothing for archaeologists to examine. Former things will be a distant memory.

> And he said unto me, It is done. I am
> Alpha and Omega, the beginning and the
> end. I will give unto him that is athirst of
> the fountain of the water of life freely.
> (KJV The Revelation 21:6)

Alpha is the first letter of the Greek alphabet, Omega, the last. We might say that Jesus is everything from A to Z. One way to look at the succession of realities, through which the saved have passed, is to view them as a process through which God has created living souls that are suitable for an eternal life in the presence of the Trinity.

> All who are victorious will inherit all these
> blessings, and I will be their God, and they
> will be my children.
> (NLT The Revelation 21:7)

God made us "in His image". He wanted us to have the experiences through which we have lived. All the troubles and emotions that we have encountered, as we have walked the narrow path to Glory, will culminate in a precious relationship with our Father.

> But the cowardly, the unbelieving, the vile,
> the murderers, the sexually immoral, those
> who practice magic arts, the idolaters and
> all liars — they will be consigned to the
> fiery lake of burning sulfur. This is the
> second death. (NIV The Revelation 21:8)

We who are saved will not experience the "second death", because we have been born twice, as we discussed earlier. Still, it is alarming to read this list of sins, for surely You and I have committed some of them. Remember, one unforgiven sin will cause You to suffer this second death, but, if You take Your sins to Jesus, and, in prayer, place them on Him, He...

> ...is faithful and just and will forgive us our sins and purify us from all unrighteousness. (NIV I John 1:9)

Being sin-free, we will escape the second death.

> One of the...angels...said to me, "Come, I will show you the bride, the wife of the Lamb." And he carried me away in the Spirit to a mountain great and high, and showed me the Holy City, Jerusalem, coming down out of heaven from God. (NIV The Revelation 21:9-10)

Often, the Bible speaks of Jesus as the Bridegroom and the Church as His Bride. In this context, the Church is the assemblage of all true-believers of all time, both Old Testament saints and New Testament saints. Now, in this passage, the New Jerusalem is called the Lamb's wife, the Bride. Is the Bride the Church or is the Bride the New Jerusalem? If we reflect on the matter, we understand. The Holy City will be composed of 2 entities: wonderful structures and wonderful citizens. Both are needed to create a Holy City. The Church will provide the inhabitants. This passage depicts the structures God has prepared for His Church. As Jesus said...

> In my Father's house are many mansions...
> (KJV John 14:2)

The Church and the structures will be lovely. In the famous "wedding passage" in the Apostle Paul's letter to the Church at Ephesus, Paul saw the bride and the bridegroom as echoes of the relationship between Christ, the Bridegroom, and the Church, the Bride. He wrote...

> ...husbands...love your wives, just as Christ
> loved the church. He gave up his life for
> her to make her holy and clean, washed by
> the cleansing of God's word. He did this to
> present her to himself as a glorious church
> without a spot or wrinkle or any other
> blemish. Instead, she will be holy and
> without fault. (NLT Ephesians 5:25-27)

So, we see the Church that inhabits the New Jerusalem will be without blemish. Likewise, John, in the following verse from The Revelation, was awed by the beauty of the structures of the Holy City...

> It shone with the glory of God, and its
> brilliance was like that of a very precious
> jewel, like a jasper, clear as crystal.
> (NIV The Revelation 21:11)

You have seen beautiful displays of precious stones here on Earth. But, the sight of this Holy City will be dazzling. The whole city will gleam as a perfect, huge jewel. And, everywhere You look, You will see gorgeous geometric patterns of precious materials. In our present bodies, probably, we could not survive in such splendor, but, then, all the saved residents will be in resurrection bodies. The city John saw in his vision was breathtaking. It...

> ...had a great, high wall with twelve gates,
> and with twelve angels at the gates. On the
> gates were written the names of the twelve
> tribes of Israel. There were three gates on
> the east, three on the north, three on the
> south and three on the west.
> (NIV The Revelation 21:12-13)

145

These 12 gates on the sides of this four-square city will be much larger than any ever built in prior realities. Each gate will be beautifully embossed with the name of one of the 12 tribes of Israel and attended by a welcoming angel.

> And the wall of the city had twelve
> foundations, and in them the names of the
> twelve apostles of the Lamb.
> (KJV The Revelation 21:14)

The foundation of the city will be 12 segments set to frame the 12 gates. They will be named for the 12 Apostles. I presume that the name "Judas" will not be found there. Probably, it will be replaced by "Matthias", who was selected to replace Judas after the Resurrection of Jesus. (Acts 21:6)

John continued...

> The angel who talked to me held in his
> hand a gold measuring stick to measure the
> city, its gates, and its wall. When he
> measured it, he found it was a square, as
> wide as it was long. In fact, its length and
> width and height were each 1,400 miles.
> (NLT The Revelation 21:15-16)

The city will be a cube, sitting on the New Earth. Consider its magnitude. Mount Everest, our highest mountain, is about 29000 feet high. It rises less than 6 miles above sea level. Generally, we think of outer space beginning at about 50 miles above the surface of the Earth. But, this city will reach far into outer space. Will we need spacesuits to visit its highest points? I doubt it. We will be in resurrection bodies, designed for the new environment. In fact, I look forward to visiting far distant objects in the New Heavens without wearing protective attire.

> Then he measured the walls and found
> them to be 216 feet thick...The wall was
> made of jasper, and the city was pure gold,
> as clear as glass. The wall of the city was
> built on foundation stones inlaid with
> twelve precious stones: the first was jasper,
> the second sapphire, the third agate, the
> fourth emerald, the fifth onyx, the sixth
> carnelian, the seventh chrysolite, the eighth
> beryl, the ninth topaz, the tenth
> chrysoprase, the eleventh jacinth, the
> twelfth amethyst. The twelve gates were
> made of pearls — each gate from a single
> pearl! And the main street was pure gold,
> as clear as glass.
> (NLT The Revelation 21:17-21)

The array of precious metal and stones will be without precedent. Of especial noteworthiness will be the pearl gates. Only God could have conceived of pearls this big. And, it will be delightful to see the transparent, golden streets.

> I did not see a temple in the city, because
> the Lord God Almighty and the Lamb are
> its temple. The city does not need the sun
> or the moon to shine on it, for the glory of
> God gives it light, and the Lamb is its
> lamp. (NIV The Revelation 21:22-23)

The Father and the Son will be, somehow, the Temple of the Holy City. Wherever they go, they will be the Holy of Holies. The Holy Spirit will continue to dwell within each saved soul. They will be temples of the Holy Spirit. The Father and Son will emit great quantities of brilliant light; so much, that they will illuminate everything on the New Earth. This hints at a novel attribute of the final reality. In our present "Here and Now" reality, the brightest light cannot illuminate sites on the other side of the Earth. But, in the last reality, the light of God will circumnavigate the globe. Perhaps, it will reflect off a new layer of atmosphere that encircles the Earth. Or, ponder this: if You study Genesis, You will note that God made day and night before He created the sun and the moon. For sure, God knows how to illuminate the whole Earth simultaneously.

> The nations will walk by its light, and the kings of the earth will bring their splendor into it. (NIV The Revelation 21:24)

Some citizens of this last reality will live outside of Jerusalem. Groups of the saved will form kingdoms, for we read, here, of the kings of the Earth visiting the Holy City.

> Its gates will never be closed at the end of day because there is no night there. And all the nations will bring their glory and honor into the city.
> (NLT The Revelation 21:25-26)

Many things will be different from what we experience in our present reality. No one will place a lock anywhere. There will be no crooks there. The gates will be ornamental and will never be closed for defensive purposes. There will never be an attack from an evil clan.

> Nothing impure will ever enter it, nor will anyone who does what is shameful or

deceitful, but only those whose names are
written in the Lamb's book of life.
(NIV The Revelation 21:27)
Only the saved will live in this new city. There will
be no coarse language. No porn. No puffed-up
elite; just those dear souls whose names are written
in the Lamb's Book of Life.

Then the angel showed me the river of the
water of life, as clear as crystal, flowing
from the throne of God and of the Lamb
down the middle of the great street of the
city. On each side of the river stood the
tree of life, bearing twelve crops of fruit,
yielding its fruit every month. And the
leaves of the tree are for the healing of the
nations. (NIV The Revelation 22:1-2)
Perhaps, You have visited a clean, clear mountain
stream. If so, You must have felt compelled to taste
of it. Well, this "water of life" will be even more
alluring. It will flow from the throne of God. The
main street of the city will be a divided pathway
with the pure river coursing through the median
strip. It will be wonderful to walk along this
thoroughfare. Here, we will see the "tree of life". It
may be something like a banyan fig tree with
multiple trunks supporting a maze of lovely
branches bearing leaves and fruit. And, since it will
occupy both sides of the river, its foliage will span
the river, making the whole median a pleasant place
to enjoy the fruit the tree produces. It will be a
huge tree, covering a vast area, for millions will
come to gather its produce. Apparently, our
heavenly bodies will need nourishment. We will
drink the living water. We will eat of the 12 fruits,

and, perhaps, we will drink a tea made from the leaves of the tree to maintain our well-being.

> And there shall be no more curse: but the
> throne of God and of the Lamb shall be in
> it; and his servants shall serve him: And
> they shall see his face; and his name shall
> be in their foreheads.
> (KJV The Revelation 22:3-4)

The curse that has plagued mankind since the days of Adam will be erased. Gone will be the predatory behaviors of former realities. No creature will eat the meat of another. Gone will be the relentless struggle for shelter and food. Working for the Lord will be exhilarating. Gone will be the language barriers imposed at Babel. Communication will be easy. None of Earth's residents will seem strange to us. Diseases and disabilities will be gone. Everyone will be healthy. Gone will be the barriers and jealousies imposed by sexuality. All will be close friends. And, each of us will regard the Lord as our closest Friend. The veil that separates us from God, now, will be lifted. We will see His face, and, in some artful way, we will bear His name on our foreheads. This will be a beautiful seal testifying that we belong to Him.

> There will be no more night. They will not
> need the light of a lamp or the light of the
> sun, for the Lord God will give them light.
> And they will reign for ever and ever.
> (NIV The Revelation 22:5)

What a privilege it will be to live and reign over the New Earth, with the Lord, forever and ever!

Yes, God created these nine realities with His ultimate goal in mind. He developed this plan to bring into Heaven a people who, while enduring the tribulations of the Earth, chose Him to be their Lord. While You have breath, You, too, can decide to place Your faith in Jesus. He wants to Boost You into the "New Heaven and Earth".

Presently, You and I are locked in the 4 dimensions of our era: length, width, height, and time. What will it be like to see the ultimate reality? finally, to comprehend the mysterious "curves" in our present reality? Only those who make it to Heaven will ever know the answers to the riddles of our Universe.

Boost Six

Jesus Wants to Give You a More Abundant Life, Now and Forever

Christ wants to lift You up, to give You a Boost into a better life, an Eternal life. He wants a closer relationship with You. He is eager to give You the "abundant life" that He often offered to His followers. To get it, You must become a part of the Family of God. Right now, Jesus is knocking on the door of Your heart. He is saying to You...

> ...I stand at the door and knock. If you hear my voice and open the door, I will come in, and we will share a meal together as friends. (NLT The Revelation 3:20)

Why not let Jesus in? He wants to be involved in every aspect of Your life, even in the routine activities, like the breaking of bread. Think about it. The very One who spoke the world into existence wants to spend time with You. He made You. He loves You. He wants to dwell in You. Surely, You would be thrilled to meet and shake the hand of the President of the United States. How much more breathtaking would it be to have the omnipotent Lord come into Your heart to stay?

The Second Birth

Christ is urging You to be "born again", not physically, but spiritually. Long ago, one night in Jerusalem, Jesus met with a fine gentleman who was attracted to Him by His Miracles and His Message. Even though Nicodemus was a prominent religious leader among the Jews, he sought guidance from Jesus. He wondered, "How does one get in to Heaven?" He was convinced that Jesus came from God, so he brought his question to Him. He got the answer in a surprising dialog detailed by the Apostle John...

> Jesus answered, Verily, verily, I say unto thee, Except a man be born of water [the natural birth that is accompanied by a gush of water] and of the Spirit [an awakening of one's spirit by the Holy Spirit], he cannot enter into the kingdom of God. That which is born of the flesh is flesh [the water birth]; and that which is born of the Spirit is spirit [the second, spiritual birth]. [Nicodemus was quite surprised by Jesus' words. He wondered how one could be "born again". Jesus continued...] Marvel not that I said unto thee, Ye must be born again. The wind bloweth where it listeth [rests], and thou hearest the sound thereof, but canst not tell whence it cometh, and whither it goeth: so is every one that is born of the Spirit. (KJV John 3:5-8)

If You are "born again", the Holy Spirit will become Your inner light, Your counselor, and Your guide. You will stop acting in the way the world expects You to act and thinking as the world expects You to think. Your world-view will change, dramatically. To the worldly, You will seem to be as unpredictable as the wind.

The thought of living as directed by the Holy Spirit may worry You as You consider becoming a Christian. To say, "Jesus is the Lord of my life" is to acknowledge that He has the right to lead You where He chooses. The Lord will be Your "boss". You will be His follower. But, keep in mind that You will be surrendering Yourself to the kindest Person in the Universe. He is infinitely kind. He is Your Biggest Booster. Jesus wants You to have an "abundant life". You will find that it is delightful to follow Him.

We wonder how Nicodemus reasoned as he pondered what Jesus had said. He was well-established. He was a "ruler" of the Jews. Perhaps, these thoughts raced through his mind: "What if the Spirit tells me to resign my prestigious post in Jerusalem and move to a small village and serve as a rabbi in a rural synagogue? Must I go? Well, yes. There may be a certain little boy in that village who needs the education I could provide to him. This change would baffle my wife and my children and all the elite of Jerusalem." Well, we know that Nicodemus did surrender his life to Christ, but the Lord kept him in Jerusalem. He stood up for Jesus when the other rulers urged that Jesus be put to death. And, he and another believer, Joseph of Arimathaea, were the men who took Jesus' body from the Cross and laid Him in His tomb.

Jesus wants You to become a "baby" Christian. He wants You to grow up in the Family of God. In our present reality, that Family is found in the Church.

If You choose to honor Jesus' wish, You will become a child of God and inherit the treasures stored up in Heaven. As the Apostle Paul put it...
> ...all who are led by the Spirit of God are
> children of God. So you have not received
> a spirit that makes you fearful slaves [to a

worldly life-style]. Instead, you received
God's Spirit when he adopted you as his
own children. Now we call him, "Abba,
Father." For his Spirit joins with our spirit
to affirm that we are God's children. And
since we are his children, we are his heirs.
In fact, together with Christ we are heirs of
God's glory... (NLT (Romans 8:14-17)

People often envy those who inherit riches here on
Earth, but the grandest bequest looks trivial when
compared to the glorious array of treasures awaiting
the saved in Heaven. The Apostle Paul taught...
 ...No eye has seen, no ear has heard, and
 no mind has imagined what God has
 prepared for those who love him.
 (NLT I Corinthians 2:9)
What will it be like to step into Heaven? Some
have compared it to a former caterpillar breaking
out of its cocoon to soar above the meadows and
trees as a beautiful butterfly. I think it will be even
more glorious than that, because none of us can
imagine how wonderful it will be. From the
Scriptures, we know we will be using our much
improved voices to sing praises to God. We will be
smarter, better looking, free from fear, surrounded
by delightful friends and relatives, walking through
a paradise of flowers and trees, drinking from
streams of crystal-clear water, and eating delicious
fruits from the flora of Heaven, as we are bedazzled
by the fountains and the golden streets and by the
jeweled structures we will inhabit. But, obviously,
these enticing glimpses of Glory are just a small
part of the whole story. I hope You want to be there
as much as I do.

The Indwelling Holy Spirit

As a down-payment on the spectacular, future inheritance You will receive if You are "born again", the Holy Spirit will take up residence within You. When Jesus walked on Earth, He was a great comfort to His apostolic team. They knew they were with God when they were with Him. When He was about to return to Heaven, He promised to send another "Comforter" to abide with His followers in His absence. The Apostle John recorded His pledge...

>...I will pray [to] the Father, and he shall give you another Comforter, that he may abide with you for ever; Even the Spirit of truth; whom the world [the unredeemed citizens of Earth] cannot receive, because it [they] seeth him not, neither knoweth him: but ye know him; for he dwelleth with you, and shall be in you. (KJV John 14:16-17)

If You receive the Holy Spirit, He will comfort You when stress comes Your way. And, since He is the "Spirit of Truth", He will open unto You the meaning of the Scriptures. The Apostle John, captured these words of Jesus...

>...when...the Spirit of truth, comes, he will guide you into all the truth. He will not speak on his own; he will speak only what he hears [spoken by the members of the Godhead in the celestial courtroom], and he will tell you what is yet to come. He will glorify me because it is from me that he will receive what he will make known to you. (NIV John 16:13-14)

This prediction was richly fulfilled. After Jesus ascended into Heaven, some of the Apostles who heard Him make this prophecy and other early Christians, wrote the New Testament. Therein, they expressed many teachings given to them by the Holy Spirit. And, they explained many Old Testament prophecies. They even added many new prophecies to the Holy Book. Also, note the amazing point made by Jesus: the Holy Spirit will participate in conversations with the Father and the Son while He is guiding You on Earth.

The Apostle Paul informed us that You and I are a composite of a body, a soul, and a spirit...

> ...I pray God your whole spirit and soul
> and body be preserved blameless unto the
> coming of our Lord Jesus Christ.
> (KJV I Thessalonians 5:23)

We comprehend the "body" more easily than the other components of our beings. It is visible and substantial, while the spirit and soul are invisible and ethereal. I believe the "soul" is what we call "personality", and the "spirit" refers to what we call "conscience". Now, these are not precise definitions, because we do not really know how to separate these three components. But, I believe the soul animates the body, while the spirit offers counsel to the "body and soul" combination. Our ability to be exact while discussing these entities is further complicated by the informal way the New Testament writers referred to them. At times, in Scripture, "soul" and "spirit" are used to refer to both of these invisible components of our beings.

If You become a Christian, You will add a fourth component to Yourself, the presence of the Holy Spirit. "He dwelleth with you, and shall be in you", as we learned earlier. He will comfort You as You face life's troubles and supply divine counsel to the other three parts of Your being.

So, Christians have 4 components in their beings. In contrast, unbelievers have either 3 or 2. Let me explain. Of course, every babe begins life with a body, a soul, and a spirit. But, the Apostle Peter warned us to...

> ...abstain from fleshly lusts, which war against the soul... (KJV I Peter 2:11)

As babes mature, they are attracted to fleshly lusts, and these can damage the spirit within them. Paul indicated that this "war" can go so far as to kill the spirit. Writing to Christians, he said...

> Once you were dead because of your disobedience and your many sins. You used to live in sin, just like the rest of the world, obeying the devil — the commander of the powers in the unseen world. He is the spirit at work in the hearts of those who refuse to obey God.
> (NLT Ephesians 2:1-2)

So, most adults are spiritually "dead". Their composite beings are reduced to 2 components. Ordinarily, the spirit may be revived by the Holy Spirit, and the unbeliever may be restored to believer status, with 4 components. However, the Scriptures do speak of a class of individuals who have resisted Christ so resolutely that they can never be redeemed. The Apostle John quoted Jesus, saying...

[God has]...blinded their eyes, and
hardened their heart; that they should not
see with their eyes, nor understand with
their heart, and be converted, and I should
heal them. (KJV John 12:40)
These miserable mortals have been permanently
reduced to 2 components. They are "spiritless
zombies", living only to satisfy their flesh and their
personalities (souls). They have been judged
already. They have no hope of reaching Heaven.

In stark contrast to these "spiritless zombies", if
You ask Jesus into Your heart, He will turn You
into a temple of God, a residence of the Holy Spirit.
Here is what the Apostle Paul said as he was
scolding the Corinthian Christians for exhibiting
some shameful behaviors...
Know ye not that ye are the temple of God,
and that the Spirit of God dwelleth in you?
If any man defile the temple of God, him
shall God destroy; for the temple of God is
holy, which temple ye are.
(KJV I Corinthians 3:16-17)
What a great privilege awaits You. You may have
God's Spirit dwelling in You.

Blessed Assurance

If You accept Jesus as Your Lord, You will have
the blessed assurance that You are saved and
Heaven-bound. You will know that Jesus is
protecting You, even holding You in the palm of
His mighty hand. Nothing will be able to pull You
out of the Savior's grasp. The Apostle John noted
Jesus' memorable words on this matter...

> My sheep hear my voice, and I know them,
> and they follow me: And I give unto them
> eternal life; and they shall never perish,
> neither shall any man pluck them out of
> my hand. My Father, which gave them [to]
> me, is greater than all; and no man is able
> to pluck them out of my Father's hand.
> (KJV John 10:27-29)

You may rest assured that Your salvation is certain.
Notice that Jesus indicated that if we are in His
hand, we are in the Father's hand. The Father and
Son are One. And, once You join the flock, You
are "in", forever. You "shall never perish". No
force can remove You from the grasp of the
Almighty.

Also, the writer of Hebrews encouraged his
Christian readers with this assertion from Jesus...

> ..."Never will I leave you; never will I
> forsake you." So we [Christians may] say
> with confidence, "The Lord is my helper; I
> will not be afraid. What can mere mortals
> do to me?" (NIV Hebrews 13:5-6)

If You become a child of God, You will never be
separated from Jesus.

A Life of Prayer

Prayer will become a central part of Your daily
activities, if You become a believer. It will be Your
opportunity to discuss Your day with Jesus. You
will thank Him for the many blessings of the day,
and ask Him for help with Your problems and
burdens. The very One who put the "curses" of
Eden, Babel, and the Flood on our civilization,
knows that You will need His help in walking

through this world of woes. Just before He went to
the Cross, Jesus gave a final Message to His
Apostles. In it He said...

> I have told you these things, so that in me
> you may have peace. In this world you will
> have trouble. But take heart! I have
> overcome the world. (NIV John 16:33)

The key phrase in this verse is "in me". When You
become a Christian, You are part of the "Body of
Christ". You are "in Christ". There, You will find
peace in a troubled world.

Christ wants to help You with Your burdens. If
You bring them to Him in prayer, He will help You.
He proclaimed...

> Come unto me, all ye that labour and are
> heavy laden, and I will give you rest. Take
> my yoke upon you, and learn of me; for I
> am meek and lowly in heart: and ye shall
> find rest unto your souls. For my yoke is
> easy, and my burden is light.
> (KJV Matthew 11:28-30)

Here, Christ promised that if You put Your energy
into His work, here and now, if You accept His
yoke and become a member of His team, He will
give rest to Your soul. Your burdens will be lifted.
But, how do You go to work for Jesus? Well, You
find like-minded believers, and together You
organize efforts to take Christ's Message to the
world. Oxen grazing in a field will not get any
work done till they are organized by yokes and reins
into a team. Then, they can do amazing work. So,
believers must be organized into teams. This is
done in well-run Churches. You need to locate a
strong Church body. There You will learn all about
Christ through its teaching services and other

activities and by reading many useful books written by Christian authors. How wonderful it is to grasp that the One who hung the stars in space has a "meek and lowly" attitude in His heart and that He wants to lighten Your burdens! You will delight in working within His team.

What about temptations? The world, the flesh and the Devil will not go mute and weak, if You become a Christian. But, if You take Your temptations to Christ in prayer, You will have the Lord and His angels watching over You. The Apostle Paul put it this way...

> No temptation has overtaken you except what is common to mankind. And God is faithful; he will not let you be tempted beyond what you can bear. But when you are tempted, he will also provide a way out so that you can endure it.
> (NIV I Corinthians 10:13)

For sure, temptations are defeated by prayer. The Holy Spirit within and the Father and Son above will guide You as You escape temptations.

When tough times come and You are very sad, if You become a Christian, You will know that all things are working together for Your good. Through prayer, You will gain the strength You need to deal with Your problems. Satan will urge You to complain to God and, if possible, to get You to blame God for Your woes. But, the Scriptures assure us that God is always watching over us. He will be working for Your good, even when You feel dispossessed. The Apostle Paul addressed this truth in his letter to the Church at Rome...

> ...we know that all things work together for
> good to them that love God, to them who
> are the called... If God be for us, who can
> be against us? Who shall separate us from
> the love of Christ? shall tribulation, or
> distress, or persecution, or famine, or
> nakedness, or peril, or sword?...I am
> persuaded, that neither death, nor life, nor
> angels, nor principalities, nor powers, nor
> things present, nor things to come, nor
> height, nor depth, nor any other creature,
> shall be able to separate us from the love
> of God, which is in Christ Jesus our Lord.
> (KJV Romans 8:28-39)

The Holy Spirit aspect of the Godhead will be in
You, forever, once You are "born again", so how
could You be separated from God. We all face
troubles here on Earth. We are not in Heaven, yet,
but, someday, all our heartaches will be behind us.
Till then, we must face our problems bravely,
keeping our focus on our future rewards.

Still, You should pray for relief from the
tribulations You encounter. Jesus taught us to do
so. He said...

> Ask and it will be given to you; seek and
> you will find; knock and the door will be
> opened to you. For everyone who asks
> receives; the one who seeks finds; and to
> the one who knocks, the door will be
> opened. Which of you, if your son asks for
> bread, will give him a stone? Or if he asks
> for a fish, will give him a snake? If you,
> then, though you are evil, know how to
> give good gifts to your children, how much

more will your Father in heaven give good
gifts to those who ask him!
(NIV Matthew 7:7-11)
Even so, we should not presume that God is a magic
genie under our control. He knows how to deliver
the "abundant life" to You. He knows the
consequences of giving You what You seek. Being
the Loving Father, He will not give You that which
will prove ruinous to You.

Suppose You are at a circus with Your little
children. They have already consumed some
buttery popcorn and a sugary drink. Now, they
begin to lobby for cotton candy. Here, You draw
the line. You say, "I know you're hungry, but the
show is nearly over, and we will get some healthy
food on the way home." Just so, God considers our
requests. We may pray for one thing and get
another, and that other will be better.

If You receive the Holy Spirit, Your prayers will
have a miraculous dimension. Since the Spirit will
be in You and advising You, You will pray
remarkably well. The Spirit will mold Your prayers
into beautiful utterances prepared for the Father's
ears. The Apostle Paul gave us this information...
   ...the Holy Spirit helps us in our weakness.
   For example, we don't know what God
   wants us to pray for. But the Holy Spirit
   prays for us with groanings that cannot be
   expressed in words. And the Father who
   knows all hearts knows what the Spirit is
   saying, for the Spirit pleads for us
   believers in harmony with God's own will.
   (NLT Romans 8:26-27)

So, that stammering prayer for an aged parent near death's door, when we know not if it is best to urge God to heal or to take our loved one into Eternity, that prayer is molded by the Spirit to fit the will of God. Whatever we pray is re-phrased by the Holy Spirit to be in exact harmony with God's benevolent will.

It's Up to You

Become a believer. Then, You will feel Christ's guiding presence. You will look back and realize that Christ has been guarding You and guiding You every step of Your journey through this world. He knew You were His before You knew. King David wrote a song expressing this sentiment...

> O Lord, you alone are my hope. I've
> trusted you, O LORD, from childhood. Yes,
> you have been with me from birth; from
> my mother's womb you have cared for me.
> No wonder I am always praising you! My
> life is an example to many, because you
> have been my strength and protection. That
> is why I can never stop praising you; I
> declare your glory all day long.
> (NLT Psalm 71:5-8)

You will have the comfort of knowing that Jesus' mighty angels are employed in guarding You...

> The angel of the LORD encamps around
> those who fear him [God], and he delivers
> them. (NIV Psalm 34:7)

From the womb to the tomb, the Good Shepherd leads. In the oft-quoted 23rd Psalm, King David gave his perspective on life in the "Here and Now".

He portrayed himself as a fragile lamb, led by a beneficent Shepherd...

> The LORD is my shepherd; I shall not
> want. He maketh me to lie down in green
> pastures: he leadeth me beside the still
> waters. He restoreth my soul: he leadeth
> me in the paths of righteousness for his
> name's sake. Yea, though I walk through
> the valley of the shadow of death, I will
> fear no evil: for thou art with me; thy rod
> and thy staff they comfort me. Thou
> preparest a table before me in the presence
> of mine enemies: thou anointest my head
> with oil; my cup runneth over. Surely
> goodness and mercy shall follow me all the
> days of my life: and I will dwell in the
> house of the LORD for ever.
> (KJV Psalm 23)

It is comforting to know that the Great Shepherd of the Universe is leading You though the tough times of life and that He will, someday, solve all Your problems by taking You to His House where You will dwell forever, free from all fears.

Jesus wants You to be "born again" and become...

> ...a new creature...[for whom]...old things
> are passed away...[and] all things are ...
> new...and all things are of God...
> (KJV I Corinthians 5:17-18)

> You will begin a lifelong process of
> improvement. Having the Holy Spirit
> within, You will exhibit the fruits of the
> Spirit listed by the Apostle Paul, in his
> letter to the Christians in Galatia...

...the fruit of the Spirit is love, joy, peace,
longsuffering, gentleness, goodness, faith,
Meekness, temperance: against such there
is no law. (KJV Galatians 5:22-23)

Your conversation will change, if You accept Jesus
as Your Lord. As the Spirit leads You into more
truth, You will want to share Your ideas with
others. The Apostle John, in his Gospel, quoted
these words of Jesus...

Whoever believes in me, as Scripture has
said, rivers of living water will flow from
within them.
(NIV John 7:38)

Sparked by the Spirit within, You will take a stand
for Jesus, just as He urged believers to do...

Let your light so shine before men, that
they may see your good works, and glorify
your Father which is in heaven.
(KJV Matthew 5:16)

Christ wants You on His team. There, You will
experience the "abundant life" He loved to
mention...

...I am come that they [believers] might
have life, and that they might have it more
abundantly. (KJV John 10:10)

You ought to give Your heart to Jesus. If You do,
then the beautiful prayer, written by the Apostle
Paul, in his letter to the Christians in Ephesus will
wrap its blessings around You. Paul expressed his
wish for all believers, that...

...from his glorious, unlimited resources he
[God] will empower you with inner
strength through his Spirit. Then Christ

will make his home in your hearts as you
trust in him. Your roots will grow down
into God's love and keep you strong. And
may you have the power to understand, as
all God's people should, how wide, how
long, how high, and how deep his love is.
May you experience the love of Christ,
though it is too great to understand fully.
Then you will be made complete with all
the fullness of life and power that comes
from God. Now all glory to God, who is
able, through his mighty power at work
within us, to accomplish infinitely more
than we might ask or think.
(NLT Ephesians 3:16-20)

Give Your all to Jesus. Then, we can worship Him
together. King David urged us to do so with these
precious words...

Come, let us sing to the LORD! Let us
shout joyfully to the Rock of our salvation.
Let us come to him with thanksgiving. Let
us sing psalms of praise to him. For the
LORD is a great God, a great King above
all gods. He holds in his hands the depths
of the earth and the mightiest mountains.
The sea belongs to him, for he made it. His
hands formed the dry land, too. Come, let
us worship and bow down. Let us kneel
before the LORD our maker, for he is our
God. We are the people he watches over,
the flock under his care. If only you would
listen to his voice today!
(NLT Psalm 95:1-7)

Commendations Incorporated
322 North Main Street, Medora, Illinois 62063
618-729-9140
commendations@mail.com